The *Anniversary* SAMPLER QUILT

40 Traditional Blocks, 7 Keepsake Settings

DONNA LYNN THOMAS

C&T PUBLISHING

Text copyright © 2017 by Donna Lynn Thomas

Photography and artwork copyright © 2017 by C&T Publishing, Inc.

Publisher: Amy Marson

Creative Director: Gailen Runge

Editors: Lynn Koolish and Katie Van Amburg

Technical Editor: Del Walker

Cover/Book Designer: Kristen Yenche

Production Coordinator: Zinnia Heinzmann

Production Editor: Jennifer Warren

Illustrator: Linda Johnson

Photo Assistant: Mai Yong Vang

Hand Model: Kristi Visser

Instructional photography by Diane Pedersen of C&T Publishing, Inc., unless otherwise noted

Some design elements and select photos and illustrations (on pages 21, 27, 32, 39, 46, 53, 62, and 71) by PhotoSpin.com.

Library of Congress Cataloging-in-Publication Data

Names: Thomas, Donna Lynn, 1955- author.

Title: The anniversary sampler quilt : 40 traditional blocks, 7 keepsake settings / Donna Lynn Thomas.

Description: Lafayette, California : C&T Publishing, Inc., [2017]

Identifiers: LCCN 2017021740 | ISBN 9781617454554 (soft cover)

Subjects: LCSH: Patchwork quilts. | Quilting--Patterns. | Patchwork--Patterns.

Classification: LCC TT835 .T4288 2017 | DDC 746.46--dc23

LC record available at https://lccn.loc.gov/2017021740

Printed in China

10 9 8 7 6 5 4 3 2 1

Dedication

This book is dedicated to the love of my life, Terry Thomas. Like two roses entwined with the passage of time, we are two but one. He is my life.

Acknowledgments

Many people helped me along the way. My quilting buddies helped put together some beautiful quilt samples on extremely short notice. Cynthia Ann Burgess, Doris Brown, Barbara Eikmeier, Alice Clark, and Beth Woods amazed me when they completed totally unique quilts well under the short deadline.

And I would be remiss if I didn't thank Barb Eikmeier for her encouragement to pursue this project in the first place and to stay true to myself in its design. I took those words to heart. I so appreciate that, when asked, Barb always gently tells me what she thinks—which is not always necessarily what I want to hear. I couldn't be more grateful for her friendship.

Contents

Foreword

40 years ago I fell in love—twice. I met the love of my life and made my first quilt (for him). What wonderful years both of those passions have brought.

Certain life events are cause for celebration and remembrance. We feel the need to mark these passages of time with something concrete, something of special significance, something full of meaning and stories. What else is a quilter to do but make a quilt?

We often think of anniversaries in terms of weddings, but they are so much more. They're yearly commemorations of a life event or a milestone. Anything important is worthy of an anniversary remembrance. We can find great joy in remembering that first kiss, a life-altering decision, a birth, a graduation, an adventure, and yes— even that first quilt!

Just as the aroma of baking bread or the melody of a favorite song can transport us to a different time, so too can quilt blocks. We quilters all have our favorites that we find ourselves making over and over again and still others that are tied to important events and special memories.

I chose my favorite 40 quilt blocks and made each of them twice for *The Anniversary Sampler Quilt*. Ruby red is the color for a fortieth anniversary, so I chose to use 40 reds in assorted values, along with 40 pinks. Deciding which blocks and which red and pink prints to include was a walk back through my life, like looking through a box of old photos. Each block told a story. Each print, whether silky or coarse, from riotous scarlet to quieter burgundy and lovely pink, sent me musing upon past days. Recalling some of these stories had me in tears, while others made me laugh all over again. What treasures these memories are!

Small things intrigue me, drawing me in for a closer look. It's no different with quilts. Miniature quilts, intricate patterns, or interlocking design elements all hold special appeal for me. So it's no surprise to those who know me that the blocks in my quilt have a finished size of 6″ × 6″ (framed to 8″ × 8″). My friend Barb told me to be true to myself, and I listened.

Stories and memories of many years, whether joyful, sad, funny, or poignant, are held in each of these blocks. I'll bet some spark memories for you, too. Come join me as I celebrate 40 years of quilting and love with *The Anniversary Sampler Quilt*. What will you commemorate in a quilt of your own?

How to Use This Book

The Anniversary Sampler Quilt is a book about celebrating or commemorating events in our lives. The 40 block patterns included were carefully selected for the story they tell or the meaning they've had over the past 40 years of my life. It was tremendously hard to limit my important blocks to just 40. There were so many more I would have liked to include!

The blocks are sorted and presented in ten chapters. Each chapter has its own theme and story, as well as instructions for how to make four blocks.

Before diving into the blocks, I recommend reading General Information (page 8) and Specialty Quiltmaking Skills (page 9). These chapters will be helpful and may save you quite a bit of angst down the road.

- ◆ To help you commemorate a special event in your own unique way, there are 6 additional and completely different quilt sets (page 98) following the block chapters. There's 1 design each for a 10-year, 20-year, 25-year, 30-year, 40-year, and 50-year remembrance.

- ◆ The spaces for blocks are left blank in the alternate sets, allowing you to use whichever blocks are meaningful for your particular quilt. You can repeat one block throughout the entire quilt or use just a few blocks, making as many as needed to fill your quilt. If appliqué isn't your thing, include or replace the appliqué with embroidery or fancy quilting. The sets are meant to be templates you can use as a jumping-off point to create your own masterpiece.

- ◆ Along with each alternate set, you'll find a photo of an actual quilt based on that set. Each quilter changed and adapted her quilt to suit the event. I encourage you to do the same.

- ◆ All of the blocks are intended to be machine pieced. Some require the use of templates to cut odd shapes that aren't easily rotary cut. I hand-pieced quite a number of the blocks simply because I enjoy the process, and you may do the same if you wish. The quilt is raw-edge appliquéd with a buttonhole stitch, and the vines were made using a ¼" bias-tape maker. Choose the appliqué method you prefer.

- ◆ Pay attention to the pressing directions in the assembly instructions. Some of them may be counterintuitive, but all have been planned so that all seams that meet—including diagonal seams—will nest together nicely, making for sharp points and a smooth, flat block.

- ◆ The patterns for the projects in this book are located on the pullout (pattern pullout pages P1 and P2). *Please note that the appliqué patterns include seam allowances.*

note

This book is geared toward the intermediate quilter. If you need help with some of the skills in this book, refer to *Visual Guide to Patchwork & Quilting* (by C&T Publishing). It covers hand piecing, machine piecing, rotary cutting, and most of the specialty seams found in this book, such as curved seams, set-in seams, and partial seams.

If you need help with appliqué, there are a number of books available from C&T Publishing that cover the myriad methods of appliqué, such as *The Best-Ever Appliqué Sampler from Piece O' Cake Designs* by Becky Goldsmith and Linda Jenkins and *The Ultimate Appliqué Guidebook* by Annie Smith.

General Information

FABRICS

The red prints used in *Forty Years of Love* are from my stash spanning about 30 years, so it seemed prudent to treat them all with Retayne, a dye fixative. (It's better to be safe than sorry!) Because I prewashed all the reds with Retayne and thus preshrunk them, I also prewashed the remainder of the fabrics for shrinkage.

You won't need much more than a fat eighth (9″ × 21″) or a 10″ × 10″ square of each print for the blocks and the appliqué. Each block assembly page includes the amount of fabric you will need for each print in that block.

I used one cream solid throughout the quilt for the block piecing and appliqué, two green prints of different values for the framing strips around each block, and a third green for the vines. The leaves are made from an assortment of ten green prints.

The block cutting and assembly instructions make one block. If you are making two or more blocks, simply multiply the quantities for each instruction times the number of blocks you are making. Increase how much fabric you need for each print in the block in the same fashion.

For example, let's say you want to make two blocks. The cutting instructions for your chosen block indicate to cut 4 squares 2″ × 2″ to make the block. For two blocks, you would double the number of squares and cut 8 squares 2″ × 2″. If a 5″ × 5″ piece of fabric is needed to cut those 4 squares, you would now need 2 squares 5″ × 5″ (or a 5″ × 10″ piece) to cut two blocks.

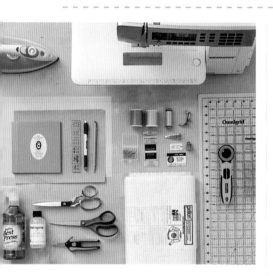

TOOLS AND SUPPLIES

A quilt of this size and scope requires a variety of supplies. You may not need all of the items listed here, depending on the methods you choose to make your quilt.

Sewing Machine
- Sewing machine in good working order

- ¼″ foot
- Open-toe foot

Cutting and Measuring Tools
- Craft scissors
- Fabric shears
- Thread snips
- Rotary cutting mat
- Rotary cutter with sharp blade
- Rotary cutting rulers
- 6″–8″ square trim-up ruler with diagonal line
- Dye fixative (such as Retayne)
- Iron
- Water spray bottle or clear starch alternative (such as Mary Ellen's Best Press)
- Template plastic, nongridded

Marking Tools
- Fine-line mechanical lead pencil
- Fine-line mechanical chalk pencil (such as those from Bohin or Sewline)
- Super fine-grit sandpaper or sandpaper board

Sewing Tools
- Threads for hand and/or machine piecing
- Threads to match prints for appliqué
- Hand-piecing needles (if hand piecing)
- Needle threader
- Sewing thimble
- Fine glass-head silk pins, 4 mm × 36 mm

Other Tools
- ¼″ bias tape maker
- Fusible web (such as the Steam-A-Seam, SoftFuse, or Wonder-Under brands)
- Hinged mirrors (such as those by From Marti Michell)

Specialty Quiltmaking Skills

In preparation for making the blocks and quilt, there are some skills that are important for you to review and learn.

MASTERING AN ACCURATE SEAM ALLOWANCE

It is important to master sewing a consistent and accurate ¼″ seam allowance. The blocks in this quilt all have a finished size of 6″ × 6″, which means some of the pieces can be quite small. This isn't a problem if your seams are accurate, but even small errors in your seam allowances can snowball into a frustrating and inaccurate end result.

You want your stitching line to be part of the ¼″ seam allowance, falling right next to that ¼″ dimension. Sometimes you'll hear this referred to as *a scant ¼″ seam* or *a quilter's ¼″ seam*.

Don't assume your seams are accurate. Test the accuracy of your ¼″ seam as follows:

1. Cut 3 strips of fabric 1½″ × 3″. Make sure the width of each strip is accurate.

2. Sew the strips together side by side along the long edges. Align the raw edges and carefully sew using the machine's ¼″ seam guide.

3. Press the seam allowances away from the center strip. The center strip should measure exactly 1″ from seam to seam.

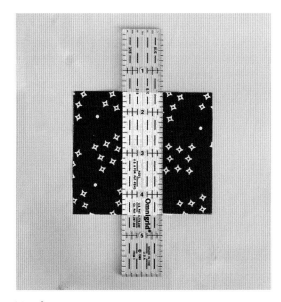

Test for ¼″ seam accuracy.

If the center strip is not exactly 1″, check your sewing habits: Were the raw edges aligned, and did you keep them aligned while stitching? Did you sew too fast to properly control the edges while stitching? Is your stitching line straight? Were the strips cut exactly 1½″ wide, or were they just "close"?

Errors in these little details are often the source of inaccurate seams. The solution is to slow down. Take the time to be careful and accurate when cutting and sewing.

Your machine could also be the problem: Does your presser foot hold the fabric layers snug enough to keep them aligned? Do the feed dogs feed fabric through without shifting layers?

If the machine does not operate properly, get it repaired. The reduction in frustration and seam ripping more than compensates for the effort.

If, despite careful stitching, the center strip still does not measure exactly 1″ wide, check the width of the seam guide itself or move your needle position to the right or left until you can sew a perfect strip test several times in a row.

OVERSIZED HALF-SQUARE TRIANGLE UNITS

Because of the small size of some of the block pieces, all the half-square triangle units in this book are cut and sewn to be oversized and then trimmed back to the correct cut size. The trim size is provided as needed in the instructions for each block.

Sewing Half-Square Triangle Units

Sew together the triangles on their long edges, sewing carefully and accurately so as not to stretch the bias. Keep your hands off the pieces as much as possible, letting the feed dogs do their work. Press the seams as indicated in the instructions.

Trimming Half-Square Triangle Units

1. Place the diagonal line of a trim-up ruler on the seam of the half-square triangle unit, with the trim-size measurement inside the lower edge of the unit.

2. Trim the top 2 edges.

3. Turn the unit around. Place the trim measurement of the ruler on the freshly cut edges and the diagonal line back on the seam. Trim the second set of edges.

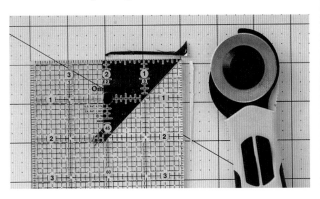

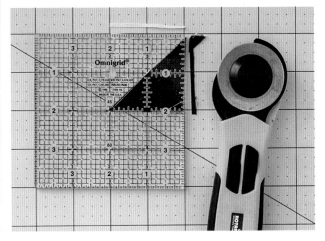

FOLDED CORNERS

Folded corners are known by multiple names, such as "the sew-and-flip method." The basic idea of folded corners is to sew a square of fabric to the corner of a larger square or rectangle along the diagonal and to fold over the smaller square to create a corner triangle. Use the following process to make folded-corner units:

1. Place the smaller square on a sandpaper board or a piece of super-fine sandpaper to keep the fabric from shifting as you mark.

2. Draw a diagonal line on the wrong side of the smaller corner square. This line must be very fine and accurate, running exactly from corner to corner. Hold your pencil at a 45° angle so that the point does not drag in the weave of the fabric.

3. Carefully place the smaller square right side down on the corner of the larger unit. Use an open-toe or clear presser foot to help you place the first corner precisely in front of the needle. Sew just to the right of the marked line so that your stitching sits next to the line, with no visible space between. Always sew with the corner that will be trimmed away positioned to the right of your needle.

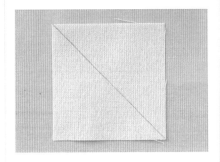

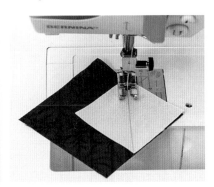

4. Press the small square back over the corner. The right side will now be facing up. Check it for accuracy (see Checking for Accuracy in Folded Corners, below).

Checking for Accuracy in Folded Corners

The square should match the corner of the larger unit exactly. If it doesn't, check the accuracy of the marked line or your sewing, and adjust as needed.

If the square comes up short of the corner, you may need to sew a thread's width closer to the corner of the unit.

If the square is too big for the corner, check to make sure you're sewing exactly from corner to corner and your pieces are lined up properly.

If there's consistent trouble, check the accuracy of the units you are starting with, the drawn line, or your sewing to find and correct the source of the problem. Each seam must be accurate in order for your final unit to finish at the size it's meant to be.

5. Trim away the 2 excess lower fabric layers ¼″ from the seam.

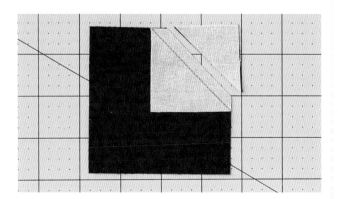

STRIPED UNITS

There are several types of striped units used in the blocks. I developed a process based on the method described in Folded Corners (previous page) to construct these units, called striped squares, striped rectangles, and striped triangles.

Striped Squares

Striped squares are made by sewing successively smaller squares onto the corners of a larger square or half-square triangle unit to create stripes. The width of the finished stripes are determined by the smaller size of each of the squares. To make striped squares, follow the steps in Folded Corners (previous page).

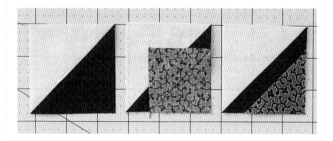

Striped Rectangles

Sewing striped rectangles is a bit different from striped squares. Rather than sewing only squares onto corners, you sew shorter rectangles onto each other to form successive stripes. You can vary the widths of stripes by shortening or lengthening the rectangle length.

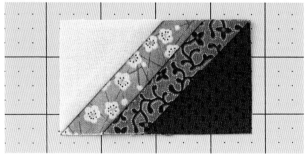

To make striped rectangles, follow these steps:

1. Sew a regular folded corner square (see Folded Corners, page 10) to the first corner of the rectangle.

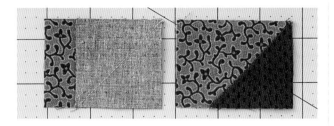

2. Mark a diagonal line on the wrong side of the rectangle that forms the first stripe. Since you can't mark from corner to corner on the rectangle to create the angle you need, you'll need to make a mark on the side of the rectangle using a square ruler with a diagonal line running across it.

Depending on the directional slant you want, place the diagonal line of the ruler on either the long leg or short leg of the rectangle.

3. Place the rectangle on the corner of the first rectangle that has the folded corner on it. Be sure to orient the diagonal line you drew parallel to the existing seam so that when the rectangle is folded over it runs parallel with the existing unit. Check to make sure it's properly aligned before sewing!

4. Sew it in place. Fold the rectangle over the corner to check for accuracy.

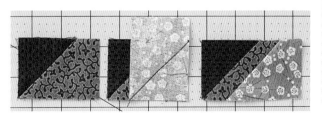

5. Trim away the excess lower layers ¼″ from the seam. Press.

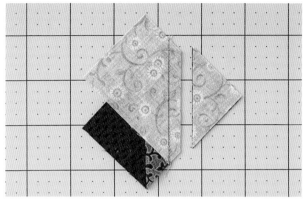

6. When all the stripes are in place, finish the unit with a folded corner on the opposite side from the first.

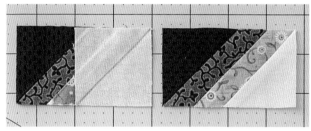

note

Be aware that because of the diagonal slant, two similar striped rectangles can be mirror images. This happens by sewing the diagonal seams on a different angle.

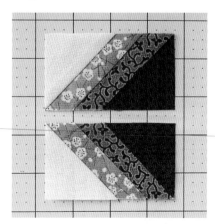

The Anniversary Sampler Quilt

Striped Triangles

There are two types of striped triangles used in this book.

The first type of striped triangle is essentially the same as a basic folded corner (see Folded Corners, page 10) on a square, except that the corner square is sewn onto the corner of a right triangle instead of another larger square.

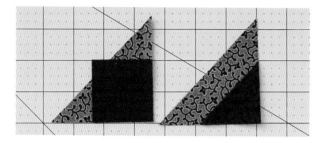

To make the second type of striped triangle, sew successively smaller triangles onto the points of a larger pieced triangle. The size of the smaller triangle determines the width of the stripe.

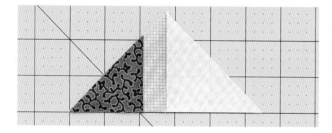

1. On the wrong side of the smaller triangle to be sewn to the larger triangle, place the line of a ruler running from the right angle (90° angle) corner to the center of the opposite long leg. Draw a vertical line.

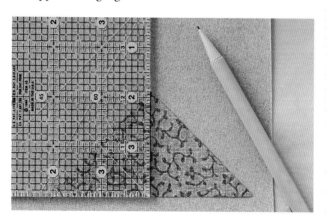

2. Place the smaller triangle right sides together on the corner of the larger triangle, and stitch on the right side of the line as you would with a regular folded corner.

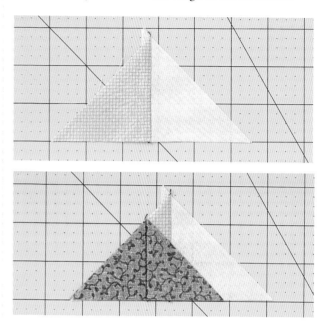

3. Fold the smaller triangle over the corner to check for accuracy. Adjust if necessary. Trim the excess lower layers ¼″ from the seam.

MAKING AND USING TEMPLATES

When you come across odd-shaped block pieces that are not easily measured and cut, the solution is to make templates that you can trace around on fabric to mark the piece.

Making Templates

Templates are made either *finished size*, without seam allowances included, or *full size*, with seam allowances included.

When you trace around a *finished-size template*, you are marking the *sewing line*. It may be a little extra work, but in some cases marking the sewing lines makes it possible to accurately cut and sew odd or funky shapes.

When you trace around *full-size templates*, you are marking the *cutting line*. That's a very distinct and important difference between full-size and finished-size templates.

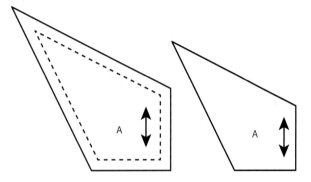

Generally speaking, *finished-size templates* are needed for hand piecing or for instances where a particular point or intersection must be perfectly matched. *Full-size templates* are used for machine piecing.

Buy good, pliable acrylic plastic to make your templates instead of using paper, which wears out quickly. A sheet of heat-resistant Mylar is okay for appliqué if you can write on it with pencil. I prefer sheets of translucent nonshiny template plastic without grids. I find the grid lines on some products too thick and visually confusing when I'm drawing shapes that don't fall on the grid lines.

To make a template, follow these steps:

1. Place the template plastic over the shape and trace. If you're drawing straight lines, mark the points with a pencil; then use a straight edge to connect the dots. For anything else, carefully trace freehand.

2. Before moving the plastic, mark each template with the designation from the pattern (for example, "A," "B," or "AR") and the grainline arrow. The side with the writing on it will be the right side of the template.

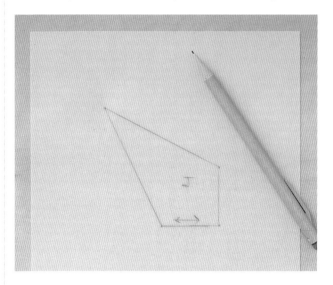

3. Cut out the templates on the lines you drew using sharp craft scissors.

note

Templates of asymmetrical shapes create mirror-image versions of themselves when you flip the template over. If you mark the template with the incorrect side faceup, you'll have the wrong image. That's why patterns are designated "AR" or "1R." The "R" stands for "Reversed."

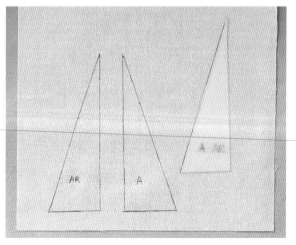

Marking and Cutting Fabric Pieces

After the templates are made, use them to mark and cut the fabric pieces.

1. Place the fabric *right side down* on a sandpaper board or a piece of sandpaper. Place the template *right side down* on the back of the fabric, aligning the grainline arrow with one of the straight grains. Trace around it. To mark reverse templates, mark with the template *right side up*.

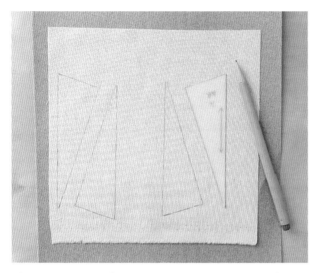

The pieces on the left were marked with the template facedown, while the ones on the right were marked with the template faceup (reversed).

2. Depending on the kind of template you are using, follow one of the sets of instructions below:

◆ **If you are working with full-size templates (seam allowances included),** mark the pieces right next to each other in a group. Cut them apart on the line with a rotary cutter and ruler or with sharp fabric shears.

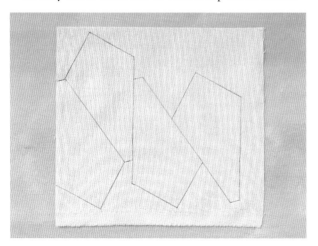

◆ **If you are working with finished-size templates (seam allowances not included),** trace around the template onto the fabric, and leave about ½″ between tracings. Cut out the pieces between the lines you drew.

Sewing Template-Marked Pieces

For pieces cut with seam allowances included, align the raw edges and sew the pieces together with a ¼″ seam allowance by machine, as usual.

For pieces marked with sewing lines, pin-match the sewing lines on the 2 pieces to be sewn instead of aligning the raw edges.

1. Spear the corner of the top piece, running the pin into the corresponding corner on the back piece. Secure the pin vertically. Repeat on the opposite corner. Pin-match the lines between the corners with 1 or 2 pins.

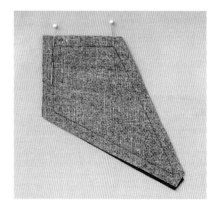

2. Hand or machine piece on the marked pencil line.

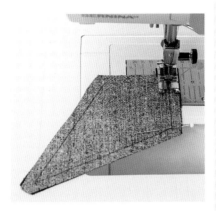

BASIC HAND PIECING

Hand piecing is different from machine piecing in one important way: You need a drawn stitching line on which to sew, since most of us can't consistently guess the placement of a ¼″ seam allowance. There are two ways to accomplish this.

Method 1: Full-Size Templates

1. Rotary cut the pieces, or use full-size templates (seam allowances included) to cut out the pieces.

2. Draw a line ¼″ from all the raw edges on 1 piece. Pin 2 pieces right sides together, matching the raw edges. Stitch on the lines as you sew the pieces together.

Method 2: Finished-Size Templates

1. Using finished-size templates (no seams included), trace around the templates and cut approximately ¼″ away from the marked lines. See Marking and Cutting Fabric Pieces (page 15).

2. Pin the first corner by spearing the point on both the front and back piece with a pin. Repeat for the opposite corner. Secure the pins vertically.

3. Use pins to match the front and back lines in the middle of the seam, using 1 pin for about every 2″ of seam.

4. Stitch from point to point on the drawn line, beginning and ending with a backstitch. When stitching, take several stitches at a time on your needle and pull through. When you take the next needleful of stitches, begin 1 stitch back. This is called a *piecing stitch*, and it is more secure than a basic running stitch.

5. Leave the seams at intersections freestanding. Backstitch at the base of the intersection when you come to it. Pass your needle through the base of the seam and across to the other side. Backstitch on this side, and continue to stitch the rest of the seam.

MAKING APPLIQUÉ STEMS

I cut bias strips to make the appliqué vines. For each quilt that requires vines there is a green print cut for this purpose. It is 18″ wide × the width of fabric for the main 80-block quilt and 11″ wide for the alternate quilt sets that use vines.

To cut bias strips, follow these steps:

1. If you are right-handed, use the 45° angle line on a ruler to make a diagonal cut from the bottom of the fabric to the upper left corner, as shown.

If you are left-handed, cut from the bottom of the fabric to the upper right corner. Set aside the corner triangle.

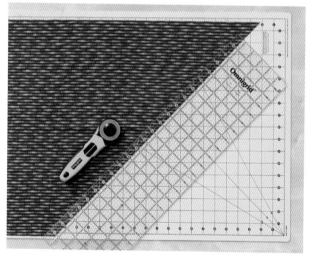

2. Cut ¾″-wide bias strips from the diagonal cut. Cut as many as indicated in the directions for the quilt you are making. You can also cut bias strips from the corner triangles if necessary.

note

To turn the bias strips into stems, I use the ¼″ bias tape maker by Clover and follow the directions on the package. I spray the strip with Mary Ellen's Best Press right before pulling it through the tape maker and then iron it as soon as it comes through the opening. This helps keep the edges securely turned under.

PARTIAL SEAMS

Some blocks don't go together in simple rows but instead are sewn around a center patch. Use partial seams to build these units around the center patch.

Notice that there are no row seams that run completely from one side to the other in this block.

Follow the steps below to get partial seams.

1. Sew half of the first seam.

2. Sew the second unit to the side of the block with the complete seam.

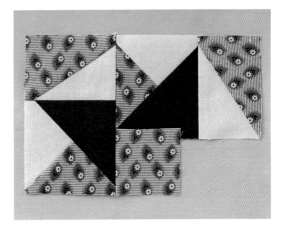

3. Continue sewing units around the center patch.

4. Sew the second half of the first seam.

THE ANNIVERSARY SAMPLER QUILT:
Forty Years of Love

Forty Years of Love; designed, pieced, and appliquéd by Donna Lynn Thomas; machine quilted by Denise Mariano

Finished block: 6″ × 6″ without framing strips, 8″ × 8″ with framing strips

Finished quilt: 91″ × 91″

*The Anniversary Sampler Quilt is made of a total of 80 blocks (2 each of 40 blocks).
The center dedication block is framed with light green, 44 blocks are framed with
a medium green print, and 36 blocks are framed with a light green print.*

Refer to The Anniversary Sampler Quilt Assembly (page 95) for the quilt assembly instructions.

---

note

The following *materials* list is for the whole 80-block quilt (each of the 40 blocks is used twice). However, the following *cutting* instructions are just for the setting. You will choose the blocks that you want to make and will refer to those specific block instructions for cutting and construction.

MATERIALS

Assorted red prints: 40 prints, each roughly between 10″ × 10″ and 9″ × 21″, for block piecing *and* appliqué

Assorted pink prints: 40 prints, each roughly between 10″ × 10″ and 9″ × 21″, for block piecing *and* appliqué

Cream solid: 7½ yards for block piecing and side setting triangles

Medium green print: 2⅝ yards for block framing strips and appliqué leaves

Light green print: 2 yards for block framing strips and appliqué leaves

Dark green print: 1¼ yards for appliqué vines and stems

Assorted green prints: 1 yard total for appliqué leaves

Fusible web: 3⅝ yards × 18″ for appliqué

Binding: ⅞ yard

Backing: 8½ yards of 40″-wide fabric *or* 2⅞ yards of 108″-wide fabric

Batting: 100″ × 100″

CUTTING

These instructions are for the setting only and do not include the individual block cutting instructions. Refer to the specific block instructions as you select and make the blocks for your quilt.

Prepare templates from patterns BB, CC, DD, EE, FF, and GG (pullout page P2).

WOF = width of fabric

CREAM

- Cut 3 strips 8½″ × 50″ along the lengthwise grain (parallel to the selvage); subcut into 2 strips 8½″ × 40½″ and 2 strips 8½″ × 24½″.

- Cut 6 strips 8½″ × WOF; subcut into 8 squares 8½″ × 8½″ and 8 rectangles 8½″ × 16½″.

- Cut 2 strips 13¼″ × WOF; subcut into 4 squares 13¼″ × 13¼″. Cut each twice on the diagonal.

- Cut 1 strip 18½″ × WOF; subcut into 2 squares 18½″ × 18½″. Cut each once on the diagonal.

- Reserve the remainder for block piecing.

MEDIUM GREEN

- Cut 9 strips 8½″ × WOF; subcut into 176 strips 2″ × 8½″.

- Reserve the remainder for the appliqué leaves.

LIGHT GREEN

- Cut 8 strips 8½″ × WOF; subcut into 148 strips 2″ × 8½″.

- Reserve the remainder for the appliqué leaves.

DARK GREEN

- Cut 2 pieces 18″ × WOF; subcut into 35–40 bias strips ¾″ wide. See Making Appliqué Stems (page 17).

ASSORTED GREENS

- Cut a total of 80 using Template CC.

- Cut a total of 144 using Template DD.

ASSORTED REDS

- Cut a total of 44 using Template BB.

- Cut a total of 96 using Template EE.

ASSORTED PINKS

- Cut a total of 44 using Template GG.

- Cut a total of 96 using Template FF.

BINDING

Cut 12 strips 2¼″ × WOF.

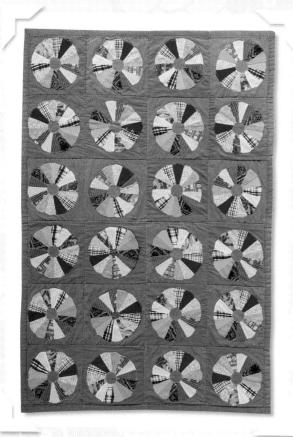

My first quilt. Embroidered in the center of the bottom plates are the words "First Attempt, October 9, 1975." Notice how poorly the polyester loft held up—but what's most appalling is that I actually wore clothes made from those fabrics!

Falling in Love

It all started in 1975. As a budding horticulture major, I found a job at a local landscape nursery. One of only two young women employed there, I worked in the retail market as well as the growing fields. If you've ever been to southeast Pennsylvania, you know that summers are hot and humid—but I loved "playing in the dirt" just the same.

There was an awful boy who worked on the landscape crews. When he wasn't out on jobs, he'd pick on me terribly, teasing and chasing me with the front-end loader, yipping and yelling as he charged along. At the end of the summer, to my utter shock, he asked me out on a date. I was dumbfounded. At my mother's insistence and in spite of serious misgivings, I went and surprised myself by falling completely in love with him on that first date.

After one more date, we went off to our respective colleges. His birthday was coming along in September, and since money was tight, I wasn't sure what gift I could give. Then I stumbled upon a picture of an old quilt at a used bookstore and thought, "Hmm … what if I made him a quilt?" How hard could that be? So I bought the book.

Assuming quilts had to be made from scraps, I pulled out my big bag of clothing scraps from the 60s and 70s and dug in to make a Dresden Plate quilt using the paper wedge in the book. I had all those lovely double knits and synthetic fabrics we wore back then, with nary a cotton in the crowd. Perfect for a quilt, right? Yikes—no! But I didn't know any better, so why not?

With warmth in mind, I bought polyester denim. I cut big squares, zigzagged the Dresden plates to them, sewed the squares together, put more polyester denim on the back, and—just to make sure he was good and warm—stuffed it with two extra-loft polyester battings! My little sewing machine struggled through that thing, smoking and bouncing along, but it got the job done.

And all this time later, we still have that monstrosity. …

40 years ago I fell in love twice. First with the love of my life, and second with the other passion that would carry me through that life in so many wonderful ways: quilting.

Block 1: Dresden Plate

30 years ago, primitive fabrics were all the rage in quilts and home decor. We had an abundance of woven plaids, checks, and stripes, and lots of new quilt patterns and ideas to go with them. A Dresden Plate wallhanging made entirely from woven plaid was one that caught my attention.

My very first quilt was a Dresden Plate with rounded spokes, but ten years later while sewing the primitive wallhanging, I learned how to make quick and easy pointy spokes for the first time. There's no need to turn under the edges of the points, making the plates quick to prepare.

Dresden Plates remain popular, whether with rounded spokes or pointy ones, a few spokes or many, a couple of prints or totally scrappy, and in any size from tiny to huge. How much fun is that?

MATERIALS

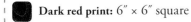 **Dark red print:** 6″ × 6″ square

 **Pink print:** 6″ × 6″ square

Very dark red print: 2½″ × 2½″ square

Cream solid: 8″ × 8″ square

CUTTING

Prepare templates from patterns A and B (pullout page P1).

DARK RED

◆ Cut 4 using Template A.

PINK

◆ Cut 4 using Template A.

VERY DARK RED

◆ Cut 1 using Template B.

CREAM

◆ Cut 1 square 6½″ × 6½″.

FRAMING STRIPS

◆ **Medium green:** Use 4 strips 2″ × 8½″ from those already cut if you are making *The Anniversary Sampler Quilt* (page 19). For any of the other quilts, please see their specific cutting instructions.

MAKE THE BLOCK

Seam allowances are ¼″ unless otherwise noted. Press all seams in the direction of the arrows indicated in the diagrams.

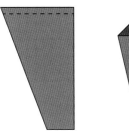 

1. Fold each wedge in half lengthwise, right sides together. Press. Stitch ¼″ from top raw edge. Turn sewn wedge right side out, easing out the point. Press each wedge flat, with seam centered down the middle on reverse side of wedge.

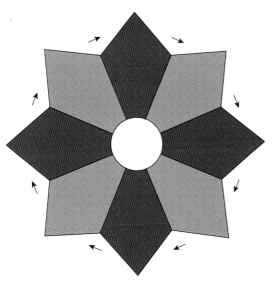

2. Sew together wedges, alternating pink and red, to form plate. Center plate, and appliqué it to cream square.

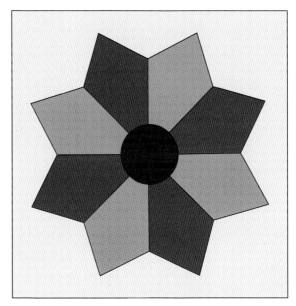

3. Prepare edges, and appliqué very dark red circle over center raw edges of plate. Appliqué circle piece B to the center.

4. Frame the block with 4 medium green strips. Trim the block to 8½″ × 8½″. See Framing the Blocks (page 96).

Block 2: Clay's Choice

After my first quilt, I realized it was time to learn how to make quilts the "right way." I bought *Let's Make a Patchwork Quilt* by Jessie MacDonald and Marian H. Schafer and set about making random blocks, learning new skills with each block. I began with hand piecing and eventually added back machine sewing, having mastered some basic concepts severely lacking from when I made that awful Dresden Plate quilt.

Clay's Choice was, and still is, a great beginner block with lots of design potential.

MATERIALS

 Dark red print: 5″ × 10″ piece

 Medium red print: 5″ × 5″ square

 Pink print: 5″ × 5″ square

 Cream solid: 7″ × 7″ square

CUTTING

DARK RED
- Cut 4 rectangles 2″ × 3½″.

MEDIUM RED
- Cut 4 squares 2″ × 2″.

PINK
- Cut 4 squares 2″ × 2″.

CREAM
- Cut 8 squares 2″ × 2″.

FRAMING STRIPS
- **Medium green:** Use 4 strips 2″ × 8½″ from those already cut if you are making *The Anniversary Sampler Quilt* (page 19). For any of the other quilts, please see their specific cutting instructions.

MAKE THE BLOCK

Seam allowances are ¼″ unless otherwise noted. Press all seams in the direction of the arrows indicated in the diagrams.

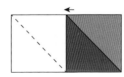

1. Draw diagonal line on wrong side of each medium red and cream square. Referring to Folded Corners (page 10), make 4 rectangle units.

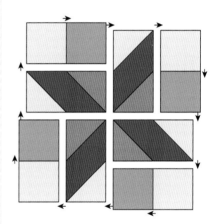

2. Sew together pink squares, cream squares, and rectangle units.

3. Frame the block with 4 medium green strips. Trim the block to 8½″ × 8½″. See Framing the Blocks (page 96).

Block 3: Churn Dash

MATERIALS

 Red print: 7″ × 7″ square

 Pink print: 6″ × 6″ square

Cream solid: 7″ × 7″ square

CUTTING

RED

- Cut 2 squares 3″ × 3″. Cut each once on the diagonal.
- Cut 1 square 2½″ × 2½″.

PINK

- Cut 4 rectangles 1½″ × 2½″.

CREAM

- Cut 2 squares 3″ × 3″. Cut each once on the diagonal.
- Cut 4 rectangles 1½″ × 2½″.

FRAMING STRIPS

- **Medium green:** Use 4 strips 2″ × 8½″ from those already cut if you are making *The Anniversary Sampler Quilt* (page 19). For any of the other quilts, please see their specific cutting instructions.

The simple Churn Dash, a perennial favorite, was included in my beginner sampler class project when I started teaching. Through these basic classes and blocks, I found I thoroughly enjoyed passing on my love of quiltmaking to others. Over the years and thousands of students later, some students still stand out.

Olive had always wanted to learn to quilt. As a child in the early 1900s, her job was to thread needles when her relatives gathered for a quilting bee, but no one ever taught her how to make the quilts themselves. She finally decided, at the tender age of 87, that it was time. She enrolled in my class and fell in love with fabric, piecing, and the creative nature of quilting. She was like a little girl again.

After a year or two, my husband and I moved on once more. Years later, I heard from the shop owner that Olive had been a steady customer and student for those last few years before she passed away. I felt so honored to have been the one to teach her something she had always wanted to learn. It's never too late to reach for our dreams, is it?

MAKE THE BLOCK

Seam allowances are ¼″ unless otherwise noted. Press all seams in the direction of the arrows indicated in the diagrams.

1. Referring to Oversized Half-Square Triangle Units (page 9), sew together red and cream triangles. Make 4 half-square triangle units. Press. Trim to 2½″.

2. Sew together cream and pink rectangles.

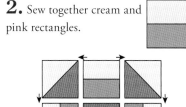

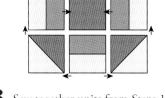

3. Sew together units from Steps 1 and 2 with red 2½″ × 2½″ square.

4. Frame the block with 4 medium green strips. Trim the block to 8½″ × 8½″. See Framing the Blocks (page 96).

Block 4: Sawtooth Star

From 1985 to 1988 I worked at A Patch of Country, a shop in Chadds Ford, Pennsylvania. Quilting was transitioning from templates to rotary cutting, and there were new ideas, books, and techniques coming through our doors on a daily basis. You never knew what innovative idea you'd learn at work on any given day. It was an exciting time in the world of quiltmaking.

The people at the shop were like family. Two of my friends, Donna and Patty, and I fell passionately in love with the gorgeous new paisleys and prints coming in from a new designer named Jinny Beyer. There had never been anything like them, and we wanted to use every last one of them in a quilt. So we got together for a sew day and made three Sawtooth Stars from each print, one for each of us. My quilt, misplaced over the years, was a treasure for a long time with all those beautiful prints and paisleys from Jinny Beyer's first collection.

MATERIALS

 Red print: 4″ × 4″ square

 Pink print: 7″ × 7″ square

 Cream solid: 7″ × 9″ piece

CUTTING

RED

- Cut 1 square 3½″ × 3½″.

PINK

- Cut 8 squares 2″ × 2″.

CREAM

- Cut 4 rectangles 2″ × 3½″.

- Cut 4 squares 2″ × 2″.

FRAMING STRIPS

- **Light green:** Use 4 strips 2″ × 8½″ from those already cut if you are making *The Anniversary Sampler Quilt* (page 19). For any of the other quilts, please see their specific cutting instructions.

MAKE THE BLOCK

Seam allowances are ¼″ unless otherwise noted. Press all seams in the direction of the arrows indicated in the diagrams.

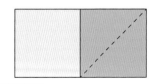

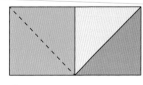

1. Draw diagonal line on wrong side of each pink square. Referring to Folded Corners (page 10), make 4 Flying Geese rectangle units.

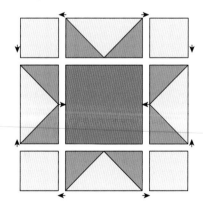

2. Sew together Flying Geese units, cream squares, and red square.

3. Frame the block with 4 light green strips. Trim the block to 8½″ × 8½″. See Framing the Blocks (page 96).

The Pleasure in the Process

After my first polyester quilt, it was obvious I needed to learn some basic skills. By using books available at the time like Let's Make a Patchwork Quilt, You Can Be A Super Quilter, and Super Quilter II, I began to learn the proper "how-tos" of quiltmaking. In the 1970s, the touted "right way" to make a quilt meant templates and hand piecing.

Back then, a nurse who could get exposed x-ray film was your best friend. This material was perfect for making long-lasting templates. Otherwise, you'd be reduced to making many, many duplicates of paper or cardboard templates that would wear out quickly with repeated use.

Quilters at that time learned how to draft, mark, cut, pin, and hand stitch their pieces. Easing in little discrepancies by hand was a breeze, especially when working with curves, set-in seams, and eight-pointed stars. None of it was the least bit intimidating by hand. I tried it all.

Then the rotary cutter stormed onto the scene, and we all jumped in full force. What heady times those were, with new ideas, skills, tools, books, and patterns arriving one right after the other!

As much as I pursued and loved those fast-cutting and machine skills, hand piecing was, and still is to this day, a glorious way to spend time. There's no rush to it. There are fewer demands and simpler tools. Within minutes you find yourself relaxing and breathing more deeply. Your heart calms and all is right with the world. You can do handwork anywhere—during kids' activities, out in the garden, while traveling, or while watching TV. As long as you can hold a little supply pouch in your lap with some ready-to-piece blocks, you can take your work with you.

The process of working so closely with the fabric, needles, and threads is the same pleasurable experience that draws others to knitting, crochet, and wool appliqué. There is a pleasure in the process of working with our hands that some of us have forgotten as quilters. Give it a try if you haven't already.

Here are a few of my favorite blocks to hand piece. See Basic Hand Piecing (page 16). You can, of course, choose to sew them by machine—in which case you'll use full-size templates to cut your pieces.

My current hand-pieced project is a Double Wedding Ring. I have no clue how big this quilt will be or when it will be done, but I'll know when I get there.

Photo by Donna Lynn Thomas

Block 5: Blazing Star

As a home economics teacher in her early years, my mother focused on garment construction. I started sewing at about age four and eventually made a lot of clothing as I grew older. But I did *not* like sewing the curves required for sleeves.

When I started quilting, I didn't think I'd enjoy curved piecing by machine any more than I did those sleeves. To conquer my fear, I tried them by hand. Well, dang if they weren't just as easy as could be! Often the slower pace and closer control of working with our hands helps us understand the special considerations required of more intimidating skills. Having conquered curves years ago, my current curved-piece project quilt, the Double Wedding Ring quilt, is a joy to sew.

Take the fear out of scary seams by trying them by hand!

MATERIALS

 Assorted red prints: 4 pieces, each 2″ × 4″

 Assorted pink prints: 4 pieces, each 2″ × 4″

 Cream solid: 6″ × 18″ piece

CUTTING

Prepare templates from patterns C, D, and E (pullout page P1).

ASSORTED REDS

◆ Cut 1 using Template C from each of the 4 prints.

ASSORTED PINKS

◆ Cut 1 using Template C from each of the 4 prints.

CREAM

◆ Cut 4 using Template D.

◆ Cut 4 using Template E.

FRAMING STRIPS

◆ **Medium green:** Use 4 strips 2″ × 8½″ from those already cut

if you are making *The Anniversary Sampler Quilt* (page 19). For any of the other quilts, please see their specific cutting instructions.

MAKE THE BLOCK

Seam allowances are ¼″ unless otherwise noted. Press all seams in the direction of the arrows indicated in the diagrams.

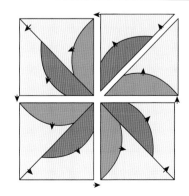

1. Sew each red piece to a cream piece E. Sew each pink piece to a cream piece D. Sew a red unit to a pink unit. Sew together the units.

2. Frame the block with 4 medium green strips. Trim the block to 8½″ × 8½″. See Framing the Blocks (page 96).

Sometimes the hardest part about a move is the knowledge that your sewing space will be the last to be unpacked and set up. Things like pots, pans, linens, and dishes take priority. I usually try to have a hand-piecing project ready for the transition to carry me through until I have a functional sewing room again.

During one move, I stitched an entire quilt top of Gentle Breeze blocks alternating with Whirling Star blocks. It provided a pleasant respite from unpacking, allowing me time to savor the beautiful, secluded, and wooded view from the back porch of our new home.

MATERIALS

 Dark red print: 4″ × 8″ piece

Medium pink print: 4″ × 8″ piece

 Light pink print: 4″ × 12″ piece

Cream solid: 4″ × 12″ piece

CUTTING

Prepare templates from patterns F and G (pullout page P1).

DARK RED

◆ Cut 4 using Template F.

MEDIUM PINK

◆ Cut 4 using Template F.

LIGHT PINK

◆ Cut 4 using Template F.

◆ Cut 4 using Template G.

CREAM

◆ Cut 4 using Template F.

◆ Cut 4 using Template G.

FRAMING STRIPS

◆ **Light green:** Use 4 strips 2″ × 8½″ from those already cut if you are making *The Anniversary Sampler Quilt* (page 19). For any of the other quilts, please see their specific cutting instructions.

MAKE THE BLOCK

Seam allowances are ¼″ unless otherwise noted. Press all seams in the direction of the arrows indicated in the diagrams.

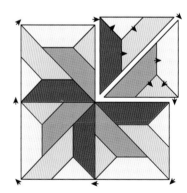

1. Sew together a dark red piece F, cream triangle, and light pink piece F. Make 4. Sew together a medium pink piece F, light pink triangle, and cream piece F. Make 4. Sew together units as shown.

2. Frame the block with 4 light green strips. Trim the block to 8½″ × 8½″. See Framing the Blocks (page 96).

Block 7: St. Louis Star

How often does this happen? You stumble onto a beautiful, you'll-die-if-you-don't-have-it print and then try to figure out what you're going to make with it. One irresistible floral with deep eggplant purple and green shouted to me from the shop shelves, inspiring me to design a quilt alternating St. Louis Star blocks with the Nosegay block (page 38). By playing with the value of the prints in the St. Louis Star blocks, a beveled effect was created. I hand pieced every last bit of that quilt, savoring the process. What fun!

MATERIALS

 Dark red print: 4″ × 8″ piece

 Medium red print: 4″ × 8″ piece

 Medium pink print: 4″ × 8″ piece

 Light pink print: 4″ × 8″ piece

 Cream solid: 10″ × 10″ square

CUTTING

Prepare templates from patterns H, HR, JJ, JJR, I, and IR (pullout page P1).

DARK RED

◆ Cut 4 using Template H.

MEDIUM RED

◆ Cut 4 using Template HR.

MEDIUM PINK

◆ Cut 4 using Template JJR.

LIGHT PINK

◆ Cut 4 using Template JJ.

CREAM

◆ Cut 4 using Template I.

◆ Cut 4 using Template IR.

FRAMING STRIPS

◆ **Medium green:** Use 4 strips 2″ × 8½″ from those already cut if you are making *The Anniversary Sampler Quilt* (page 19). For any of the other quilts, please see their specific cutting instructions.

MAKE THE BLOCK

Seam allowances are ¼″ unless otherwise noted. Press all seams in the direction of the arrows indicated in the diagrams.

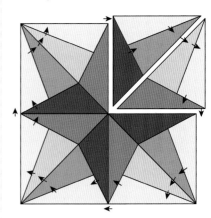

1. Sew a cream piece I to a medium pink piece JJR. Sew a dark red piece H to the bottom. Make 4. Sew a cream piece IR to a light pink piece JJ. Sew a medium red piece HR to the bottom. Make 4. Sew together assorted units.

2. Frame the block with 4 medium green strips. Trim the block to 8½″ × 8½″. See Framing the Blocks (page 96).

Block 8: Simple Star

When teaching hand-piecing skills, Simple Star is a longtime favorite. Despite its simplicity, students learn a variety of skills and concepts as they explore the slower pace devoted to the pleasure in the process.

I bet I've made a hundred of these blocks in every theme you can imagine. Whenever I'm between hand-piecing projects, I get out my Simple Star templates, some fabric, and cut and sew yet a few more variations of this old friend.

MATERIALS

 Assorted red prints: 4 squares, each 5″ × 5″

 Cream solid: 6″ × 11″ piece

CUTTING

Prepare templates from patterns J and K (pullout page P1).

ASSORTED REDS

◆ Cut 1 using Template J from each of the 4 prints.

CREAM

◆ Cut 4 using Template K.

FRAMING STRIPS

◆ **Medium green:** Use 4 strips 2″ × 8½″ from those already cut if you are making *The Anniversary Sampler Quilt* (page 19). For any of the other quilts, please see their specific cutting instructions.

MAKE THE BLOCK

Seam allowances are ¼″ unless otherwise noted. Press all seams in the direction of the arrows indicated in the diagrams.

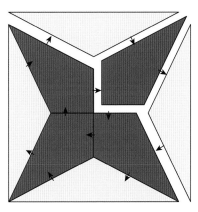

1. Sew together 4 red pieces. Add cream pieces.

2. Frame the block with 4 medium green strips. Trim the block to 8½″ × 8½″. See Framing the Blocks (page 96).

For the Love of Gardening

Gardening brought my husband and me together. We've always enjoyed designing and installing English cottage gardens, even though we've moved 21 times and rarely stayed anywhere long enough to see the gardens fully mature. Naturally, I also love making floral- or garden-related quilt blocks. Baskets, flowers, and whirligigs—anything that could go in a garden appeals to me.

Linda, a quilting buddy and fellow gardener, stitched a light and colorful version of Night Time in the Garden for one of my books. Sadly she's gone now, but my quilt, which hangs in my office, reminds me of her friendship.

Which of your quilts reminds you of someone?

Night Time in the Garden by Donna Lynn Thomas, 20″ × 44″

Block 9: Rosebud

Aah ... for a gardener, the anticipation and promise of a rosebud just about to explode into glorious beauty and heady fragrance is almost unbearable. We check every morning for that wonderful moment when the promise is finally fulfilled. Cupping the beautiful new creation in your hand and pulling it toward your nose to take in the ephemeral beauty of its scent is one of a gardener's greatest joys. All these things come to mind with this delicate block.

MATERIALS

 Red print: 4″ × 7″ piece

 Pink print: 5″ × 5″ square

 Cream solid: 7″ × 12″ piece

CUTTING

RED

◆ Cut 2 squares 2⅞″ × 2⅞″. Cut each once on the diagonal.

PINK

◆ Cut 4 squares 2″ × 2″. Cut each once on the diagonal.

CREAM

◆ Cut 2 squares 3⅞″ × 3⅞″. Cut each once on the diagonal.

◆ Cut 4 squares 2″ × 2″. Cut each once on the diagonal.

◆ Cut 2 squares 1⅞″ × 1⅞″. Cut each once on the diagonal.

FRAMING STRIPS

◆ **Medium green:** Use 4 strips 2″ × 8½″ from those already cut if you are making *The Anniversary Sampler Quilt* (page 19). For any of the other quilts, please see their specific cutting instructions.

MAKE THE BLOCK

Seam allowances are ¼″ unless otherwise noted. Press all seams in the direction of the arrows indicated in the diagrams.

1. Referring to Oversized Half-Square Triangle Units (page 9), sew together cream and pink 2″ triangles. Make 8 half-square triangle units. Press. Trim to 1½″.

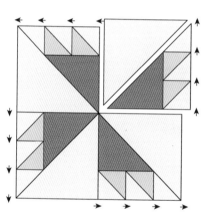

2. Sew together 1 cream 1⅞″ triangle, 2 half-square triangle units, and 1 red 2⅞″ triangle. Make 4 pieced units. Sew the pieced units to cream 3⅞″ triangles. Join together the 4 units.

3. Frame the block with 4 medium green strips. Trim the block to 8½″ × 8½″. See Framing the Blocks (page 96).

Block 10: Posy Basket

Every gardener has a gathering basket to hold clipped flowers: the narcissus of spring and the roses, lavender, and daisies of summer. Just when I think the gardens are done, late-blooming Sheffield daisies keep my basket and the bees busy well into late October with massive, swaying pink flowers that take my breath away. For years, Posy Basket quilts of some sort have graced the walls of my home.

MATERIALS

 Red print: 5″ × 7″ piece

 Medium pink print: 5″ × 5″ square

 Light pink print: 5″ × 5″ square

 Cream solid: 10″ × 10″ square

CUTTING

RED

◆ Cut 1 square 4″ × 4″. Cut once on the diagonal. You will have 1 left-over triangle if you are making 1 block.

◆ Cut 2 squares 2″ × 2″.

MEDIUM PINK

◆ Cut 2 rectangles 2″ × 3½″.

LIGHT PINK

◆ Cut 1 square 2″ × 2″.

◆ Cut 1 square 2½″ × 2½″. Cut once on the diagonal.

CREAM

◆ Cut 2 rectangles 2″ × 3½″.

◆ Cut 1 square 4″ × 4″. Cut once on the diagonal. You will have 1 left-over triangle if you are making 1 block.

◆ Cut 3 squares 2″ × 2″.

◆ Cut 1 square 2½″ × 2½″. Cut once on the diagonal.

FRAMING STRIPS

◆ **Medium green:** Use 4 strips 2″ × 8½″ from those already cut if you are making *The Anniversary Sampler Quilt* (page 19). For any of the other quilts, please see their specific cutting instructions.

MAKE THE BLOCK

Seam allowances are ¼″ unless otherwise noted. Press all seams in the direction of the arrows indicated in the diagrams.

1. Referring to Oversized Half-Square Triangle Units (page 9), sew together 2 cream and 2 light pink 2½″ triangles. Make 2 half-square triangle units. Press. Trim to 2″.

2. Sew together cream and red 4″ triangles. Press. Trim to 3½″.

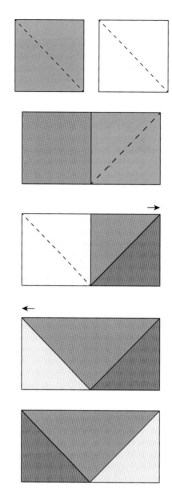

3. Draw a diagonal line on wrong side of each cream and red 2″ × 2″ square. Make 1 of each type of Flying Geese unit. See Folded Corners (page 10).

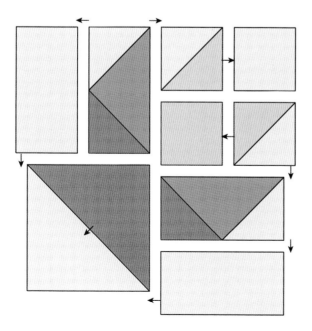

4. Sew together cream rectangles, Flying Geese units, half-square triangle units, cream square, and pink square.

5. Frame the block with 4 medium green strips. Trim the block to 8½″ × 8½″. See Framing the Blocks (page 96).

Block 11: Pansy

One of the things I love best about the Southeast is the glorious spring that is like nowhere else we've lived. Pansies are part of that beauty, along with dogwoods, redbuds, and a thousand other blooming plants. Just walking outside makes you happy to be alive.

One lovely spring afternoon when living in Peachtree City, Georgia, we planted 200 happy-faced pansies in our new gardens only to discover the next morning that our house had hosted a wildly popular Bambi salad buffet while we slept. We woke to a lot of fat and happy deer but nary a pansy in sight.

MATERIALS

 Red print: 5″ × 8″ piece

 Medium pink print: 4″ × 8″ piece

 Light pink print: 6″ × 8″ piece

 Cream solid: 10″ × 10″ square

CUTTING

RED

◆ Cut 4 squares 2″ × 2″.

◆ Cut 1 square 2½″ × 2½″. Cut once on the diagonal.

MEDIUM PINK

◆ Cut 1 square 2″ × 2″.

◆ Cut 2 squares 2½″ × 2½″. Cut once on the diagonal. You will have 1 leftover triangle if you are making 1 block.

LIGHT PINK

◆ Cut 2 rectangles 2″ × 3½″.

◆ Cut 1 square 2½″ × 2½″. Cut once on the diagonal. You will have 1 leftover triangle if you are making 1 block.

CREAM

◆ Cut 2 rectangles 2″ × 3½″.

◆ Cut 2 squares 2½″ × 2½″. Cut once on the diagonal.

◆ Cut 4 squares 2″ × 2″.

FRAMING STRIPS

◆ **Light green:** Use 4 strips 2″ × 8½″ from those already cut if you are making *The Anniversary Sampler Quilt* (page 19). For any of the other quilts, please see their specific cutting instructions.

MAKE THE BLOCK

Seam allowances are ¼" unless otherwise noted. Press all seams in the direction of the arrows indicated in the diagrams.

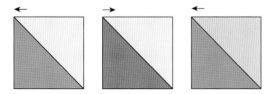

1. Referring to Oversized Half-Square Triangle Units (page 9), sew together 2 cream and 2 medium pink 2½" triangles. Sew together 2 cream and 2 red 2½" triangles. Sew together 1 medium pink and 1 light pink 2½" triangle. Trim all to 2".

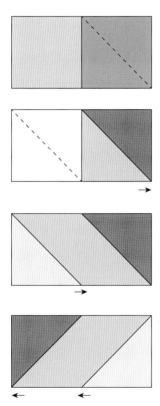

2. Draw a diagonal line on wrong side of 2 cream and 2 red 2" × 2" squares. Make 1 rectangle unit. Make a second unit that is a mirror image of first. See Folded Corners (page 10).

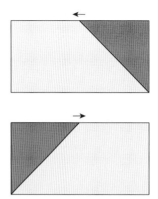

3. Draw a diagonal line on wrong side of 2 red 2" × 2" squares. Make 2 rectangle units that are mirror images. See Folded Corners (page 10).

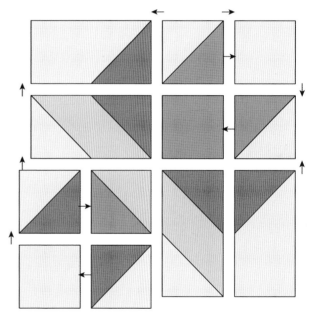

4. Sew together assorted units.

5. Frame the block with 4 light green strips. Trim the block to 8½" × 8½". See Framing the Blocks (page 96).

Block 12: Nosegay

The romance of this block's name conjures up images of warm and sultry summer weddings. Beautiful flowers abound, but the loveliest of all is saved for the bride's nosegay. Gardenias, stephanotis, sweetheart roses, white canna lilies—can't you just picture them and imagine their delicate fragrances?

Consider spending a serene summer afternoon in the garden hand piecing this lovely old block.

MATERIALS

 Dark red print: 5″ × 5″ square

 Medium red print: 5″ × 5″ square

 Medium pink print: 5″ × 5″ square

 Light pink print: 5″ × 5″ square

 Cream solid: 10″ × 10″ square

CUTTING

Prepare templates from patterns L, LR, M, N, and NR (pullout page P1).

DARK RED

♦ Cut 1 using Template L.

♦ Cut 1 using Template LR.

MEDIUM RED

♦ Cut 1 using Template L.

♦ Cut 1 using Template LR.

MEDIUM PINK

♦ Cut 1 using Template L.

♦ Cut 1 using Template LR.

LIGHT PINK

♦ Cut 1 using Template M.

CREAM

♦ Cut 1 square 4¼″ × 4¼″. Cut twice on the diagonal. You will have 2 leftover triangles if you are making 1 block.

♦ Cut 3 squares 2″ × 2″.

♦ Cut 1 using Template N.

♦ Cut 1 using Template NR.

FRAMING STRIPS

♦ **Light green:** Use 4 strips 2″ × 8½″ from those already cut if you are making *The Anniversary Sampler Quilt* (page 19). For any of the other quilts, please see their specific cutting instructions.

MAKE THE BLOCK

Seam allowances are ¼″ unless otherwise noted. Press all seams in the direction of the arrows indicated in the diagrams.

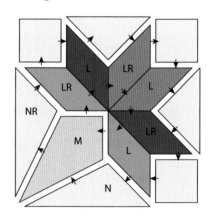

1. Sew together dark red, medium red, and medium pink pieces L and LR, and light pink piece M. Set in assorted cream pieces.

2. Frame the block with 4 light green strips. Trim the block to 8½″ × 8½″. See Framing the Blocks (page 96).

You Should Love Your Work

The 1980s were transformational years. It was a decade that began with traditional quiltmaking skills using templates and hand piecing, and ended with rotary cutting, quick piecing, and (gasp!) machine quilting.

Those days saw the start of my first small business publishing patterns and my first book, Country Schoolhouse. The book was typed on a real live typewriter (correctable back ten spaces) and illustrated with hand-drawn diagrams cut and pasted onto the master pages. The cover art was hand drawn, and the photograph of the quilt was a snapshot pasted inside the front cover.

My mother-in-law helped by transcribing each day's typing onto the newfangled word processor she used at work. Then we'd edit it at night over wine and giggles.

The book didn't go very far, but I learned a lot in the process, namely that the next time would be with a publisher. And thus I stumbled onto a totally unexpected career that continues to this day.

My first book, *Country Schoolhouse*, 1987

In the mid-80s I taught a popular Schoolhouse quilt project. Everyone was still learning about the new rotary cutter, how to sew and nest accurate seams, and all the other skills we take for granted now. My instructions included tearing strips and templates for those who didn't yet have a rotary cutter. It's entertaining to go back and read those old instructions.

The Schoolhouse block went on to become the subject of my first book, my company logo, and a miniature quilt.

MATERIALS

 Dark red print: 8″ × 10″ piece

 Medium pink print: 5″ × 5″ square

 Light pink print: 5″ × 5″ square

 Cream solid: 10″ × 10″ square

CUTTING

Sort and label all pieces by size and color to avoid confusion.

DARK RED

- ◆ Cut 1 square 2″ × 2″. Cut once on the diagonal.
- ◆ Cut 2 squares 1⅛″ × 1⅛″.
- ◆ Cut 2 rectangles 1″ × 2½″.
- ◆ Cut 2 rectangles 1⅛″ × 2″.
- ◆ Cut 1 rectangle 1″ × 2¾″.
- ◆ Cut 1 strip 1⅛″ × 4¾″.

MEDIUM PINK

- ◆ Cut 1 square 2″ × 2″. Cut once on the diagonal.
- ◆ Cut 1 rectangle 1½″ × 1¾″.

LIGHT PINK

- ◆ Cut 1 rectangle 1½″ × 2½″.
- ◆ Cut 1 rectangle 1½″ × 2″.

CREAM

- ◆ Cut 1 square 2″ × 2″. Cut once on the diagonal.
- ◆ Cut 3 rectangles 1⅛″ × 1½″.
- ◆ Cut 2 squares 3⅞″ × 3⅞″. Cut once on the diagonal.

FRAMING STRIPS

- ◆ **Light green:** Use 4 strips 2″ × 8½″ from those already cut if you are making *The Anniversary Sampler Quilt* (page 19). For any of the other quilts, please see their specific cutting instructions.

MAKE THE BLOCK

Seam allowances are ¼″ unless otherwise noted. Press all seams in the direction of the arrows indicated in the diagrams.

1. Referring to Oversized Half-Square Triangle Units (page 9), sew together dark red, medium pink, and cream 2″ triangles. Make 1 each of the 3 half-square triangle units shown. Press. Trim each to 1½″.

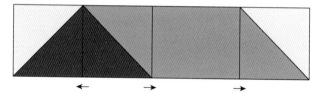

2. Sew together 3 half-square triangle units from Step 1 and 1 medium pink 1½″ × 1¾″ rectangle.

3. Sew together 2 dark red 1⅛″ × 1⅛″ squares and 3 cream 1⅛″ × 1½″ rectangles.

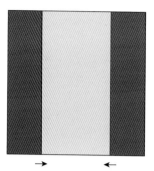

4. Sew a dark red 1″ × 2½″ rectangle to the sides of 1 light pink 1½″ × 2½″ rectangle.

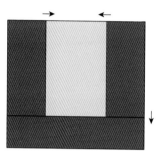

5. Sew a dark red 1⅛″ × 2″ rectangle to the sides of 1 light pink 1½″ × 2″ rectangle. Sew 1 dark red 1″ × 2¾″ rectangle to the bottom.

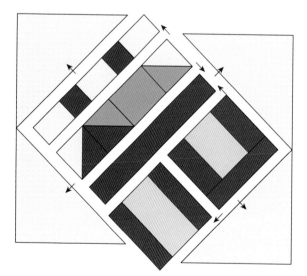

6. Sew together assorted house parts. Add 4 cream 3⅞″ triangles to the corners.

7. Frame the block with 4 light green strips. Trim the block to 8½″ × 8½″. See Framing the Blocks (page 96).

Block 14: Honey Bee

In the mid-1980s I started teaching classes at my local quilt shop, including a six-week-long basic quiltmaking class. Enjoying teaching others and encouraged by my fellow teachers, I sought to earn my National Quilter's Association Certified Teacher certificate. The first step was making a hand-pieced and hand-appliquéd Honey Bee block for scrutiny. Oh, the agony of waiting for the review and critique to come back! Would I be accepted?

I was, and two years later in 1988, I was awarded my NQACT certificate.

MATERIALS

 Red print: 5″ × 5″ square

 Medium pink print: 10″ × 10″ square

 Light pink print: 7″ × 7″ square

 Cream solid: 5″ × 10″ piece

CUTTING

Prepare a template from pattern DD (pullout page P2).

RED
- Cut 5 squares 1½″ × 1½″.

MEDIUM PINK
- Cut 12 using Template DD.

LIGHT PINK
- Cut 4 squares 1½″ × 1½″.
- Cut 4 squares 2″ × 2″.

CREAM
- Cut 4 rectangles 2″ × 3½″.

FRAMING STRIPS
- **Medium green:** Use 4 strips 2″ × 8½″ from those already cut

if you are making *The Anniversary Sampler Quilt* (page 19). For any of the other quilts, please see their specific cutting instructions.

MAKE THE BLOCK

Seam allowances are ¼″ unless otherwise noted. Press all seams in the direction of the arrows indicated in the diagrams.

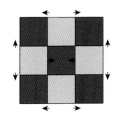

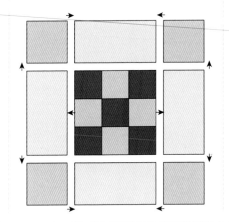

1. Sew together 5 red and 4 light pink 1½″ squares to make nine-patch units. Sew together 4 light pink squares, cream rectangles, and nine-patch unit.

2. Appliqué the medium pink pieces DD to corners of nine-patch unit.

3. Frame the block with 4 medium green strips. Trim the block to 8½″ × 8½″. See Framing the Blocks (page 96).

Block 15: Yankee Puzzle

Yankee Puzzle is an old block that transfers well to modern sensibilities. You can change its character depending on the colors or fabrics you use and the parts of the block you choose to emphasize.

Amish quilts were popular when Roberta Horton wrote her book *An Amish Adventure* (by C&T Publishing) in 1983. Shops loaded up on blacks, grays, and appropriately colored solids so we could make beautiful Amish-style quilts. I made my quilt using the Yankee Puzzle block and called it *Amish Puzzle*. Even after all these years, I haven't tired of the quilt or block.

MATERIALS

 Red print: 6″ × 8″ piece

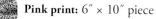 **Pink print:** 6″ × 10″ piece

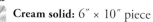 **Cream solid:** 6″ × 10″ piece

CUTTING

RED

◆ Cut 4 rectangles 2″ × 3½″.

◆ Cut 2 squares 2½″ × 2½″. Cut once on the diagonal.

PINK

◆ Cut 4 squares 2″ × 2″.

◆ Cut 2 squares 2½″ × 2½″. Cut once on the diagonal.

CREAM

◆ Cut 4 squares 2″ × 2″.

◆ Cut 2 squares 2½″ × 2½″. Cut once on the diagonal.

FRAMING STRIPS

◆ **Medium green:** Use 4 strips 2″ × 8½″ from those already cut if you are making *The Anniversary Sampler Quilt* (page 19). For any of the other quilts, please see their specific cutting instructions.

MAKE THE BLOCK

Seam allowances are ¼″ unless otherwise noted. Press all seams in the direction of the arrows indicated in the diagrams.

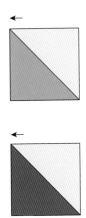

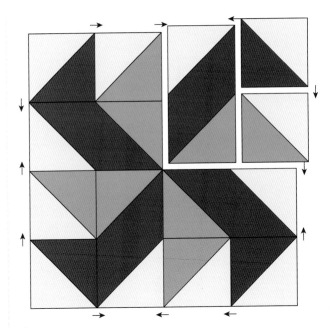

1. Referring to Oversized Half-Square Triangle Units (page 9), sew together 4 red, 4 pink, and 8 cream 2½″ triangles to make 4 each of 2 types of half-square triangle units. Press. Trim each to 2″.

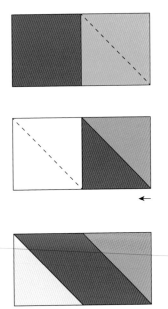

2. Draw a diagonal line on wrong side of 4 cream and 4 pink 2″ × 2″ squares. Sew them to corners of red rectangles to make 4 rectangle units. See Folded Corners (page 10).

3. Sew together half-square triangle units and rectangle units to make block.

4. Frame the block with 4 medium green strips. Trim the block to 8½″ × 8½″. See Framing the Blocks (page 96).

Block 16: Paddlestar

I enjoy setting blocks straight that create secondary designs. When Paddlestar blocks are sewn thus, a scrappy Sawtooth Star forms at the intersection. My friend Kath once made a sample Paddlestar quilt for one of my books and has been making them ever since. She uses a scrappy approach, drawing from her extensive stash and making quilts that absolutely sparkle. They're her "comfort block" to make when she just wants to sew.

MATERIALS

 Red print: 6″ × 8″ piece

 Pink print: 6″ × 8″ piece

 Cream solid: 10″ × 10″ square

CUTTING

RED

◆ Cut 1 square 3″ × 3″. Cut once on the diagonal.

◆ Cut 4 squares 2″ × 2″. Cut once on the diagonal.

◆ Cut 2 squares 1½″ × 1½″.

PINK

◆ Cut 1 square 3″ × 3″. Cut once on the diagonal.

◆ Cut 6 squares 1½″ × 1½″.

CREAM

◆ Cut 2 squares 3″ × 3″. Cut once on the diagonal.

◆ Cut 4 squares 2″ × 2″. Cut once on the diagonal.

◆ Cut 4 squares 1½″ × 1½″.

FRAMING STRIPS

◆ **Medium green:** Use 4 strips 2″ × 8½″ from those already cut if you are making *The Anniversary Sampler Quilt* (page 19). For any of the other quilts, please see their specific cutting instructions.

MAKE THE BLOCK

Seam allowances are ¼″ unless otherwise noted. Press all seams in the direction of the arrows indicated in the diagrams.

1. Referring to Oversized Half-Square Triangle Units (page 9), sew together small red and cream 2″ triangles to make 8 half-square triangle units. Press. Trim to 1½″.

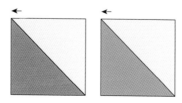

2. Sew together large red and cream 3″ triangles and pink and cream 3″ triangles to make 2 half-square triangle units of each. Press. Trim to 2½″.

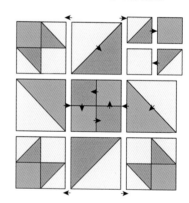

3. Sew together assorted half-square triangle units and red, pink, and cream squares.

4. Frame the block with 4 medium green strips. Trim the block to 8½″ × 8½″. See Framing the Blocks (page 96).

Oh, the Friends I've Made!

With so many military and civilian moves, I always found new friends quickly through the local quilting community.

After one move, I was out shopping to restock the kitchen and pantry for the new house. My twelve-year-old son had come along to help. We were happily strolling through the supermarket, filling two shopping carts to the brim, when I spotted a woman further down the aisle wearing a quilt-themed T-shirt. I stopped the carts and trotted over to introduce myself and find out about the quilting activities and groups in our new town.

My son just about fainted from embarrassment, turning all shades of red and slinking around to the next aisle where he could die a thousand deaths in private torment! I still laugh every time I think about it, but I found new friends that day.

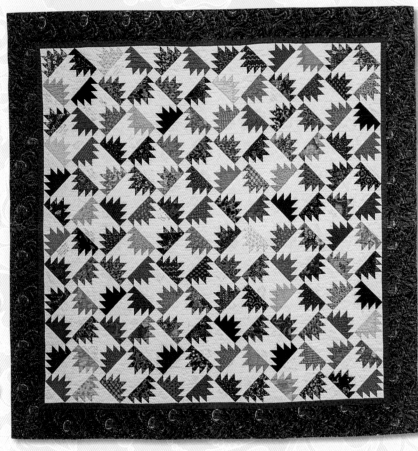

Friends and Family by Donna Lynn Thomas, 69″ × 69″

Block 17: Kansas Troubles

I have a love affair with triangles. When they're tiny, I'm even more head over heels in love with them! Kansas Troubles, Barrister block, or any of the blocks with lots of triangles make my heart go pit-a-pat.

Friends and Family (previous page) incorporates signature patches that are part of the Kansas Troubles block. About 20 years ago, I made dozens of the patches and asked friends and family to sign them. I mailed them around the country and overseas, leaving about 30 blocks unsigned for future friends and family.

They're all signed now, so I think it's time for a new signature quilt, don't you?

MATERIALS

 Assorted red prints: 4 pieces, each 5″ × 8″

 Cream solid: 10″ × 12″ piece

CUTTING

ASSORTED REDS

◆ Cut 1 square 3¼″ × 3¼″ from each of the 4 red prints. Cut once on the diagonal. You will have 1 leftover triangle from each print if you are making 1 block.

◆ Cut 3 squares 1¾″ × 1¾″. Cut once on the diagonal.

CREAM

◆ Cut 2 squares 3¼″ × 3¼″. Cut once on the diagonal.

◆ Cut 12 squares 1¾″ × 1¾″. Cut once on the diagonal.

◆ Cut 4 squares 1¼″ × 1¼″.

FRAMING STRIPS

◆ **Medium green:** Use 4 strips 2″ × 8½″ from those already cut if you are making *The Anniversary Sampler Quilt* (page 19). For any of the other quilts, please see their specific cutting instructions.

MAKE THE BLOCK PATCHES

Seam allowances are ¼″ unless otherwise noted. Press all seams in the direction of the arrows indicated in the diagrams.

Sort your pieces by red print, keeping the prints separate. Assign each red print to one of the four quadrants of the block. Two of the quadrants are pressed in the opposite direction from the other two. If the instructions are followed carefully, all seams will nest when sewing the block together.

1. Work with 1 red print at a time. Using the first red print, refer to Oversized Half-Square Triangle Units (page 9) to sew together red and cream 1¾″ triangles. Make 6. Press. Trim to 1¼″. Sew together red and cream 3¼″ triangles. Press. Trim to 2¾″.

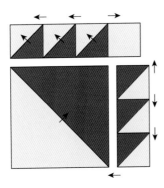

2. Sew together large half-square triangle unit, 6 small half-square triangle units, and small cream square. Pay careful attention to pressing directions.

3. Repeat Steps 1–2 with another red print. Use these 2 quarter-blocks for Quadrants 1 and 3.

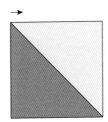

4. Make same half-square triangle units as in Steps 1–3, using another red print and *opposite* pressing directions.

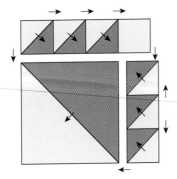

5. Sew together large half-square triangle unit, 6 small half-square triangle units, and small cream square. Pay careful attention to pressing directions.

6. Repeat with another red print. Use these 2 quarter-blocks for Quadrants 2 and 4.

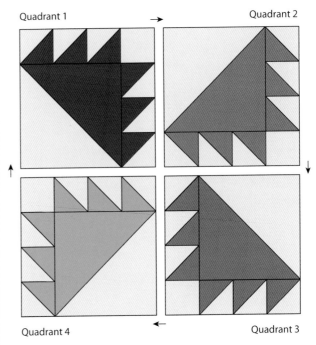

7. Sew together quarter-block units 1–4.

8. Frame the block with 4 medium green strips. Trim the block to 8½″ × 8½″. See Framing the Blocks (page 96).

Block 18: Friendship Star

What a perfect block for a friendship block exchange! Whether made with planned fabrics or a multitude of scraps, this block is easy to sew and set together into all kinds of interesting designs. Leave the center blank for signatures, or fill it with color.

A few years ago, my Wednesday morning group decided we'd each make a dozen of these blocks every month for a year and exchange them with each other. That ended up being 144 blocks for each of us—a tad over the top. Many of us are still trying to find ways to use our blocks!

MATERIALS

 Red print: 3″ × 3″ square

 Pink print: 4″ × 7″ piece

Cream solid: 10″ × 10″ square

CUTTING

RED

◆ Cut 1 square 2½″ × 2½″.

PINK

◆ Cut 2 squares 3″ × 3″. Cut once on the diagonal.

CREAM

◆ Cut 4 squares 2½″ × 2½″.

◆ Cut 2 squares 3″ × 3″. Cut once on the diagonal.

FRAMING STRIPS

◆ **Medium green:** Use 4 strips 2″ × 8½″ from those already cut if you are making *The Anniversary Sampler Quilt* (page 19). For any of the other quilts, please see their specific cutting instructions.

MAKE THE BLOCK

Seam allowances are ¼″ unless otherwise noted. Press all seams in the direction of the arrows indicated in the diagrams.

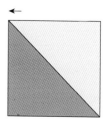

1. Sew together pink and cream triangles. Make 4 half-square triangle units. Press. Trim to 2½″. See Oversized Half-Square Triangle Units (page 9).

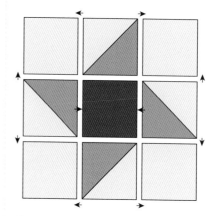

2. Sew together red square, cream squares, and half-square triangle units.

3. Frame the block with 4 medium green strips. Trim the block to 8½″ × 8½″. See Framing the Blocks (page 96).

Block 19: Album

MATERIALS

 Red print: 5″ × 10″ piece

 Pink print: 5″ × 5″ square

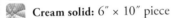 **Cream solid:** 6″ × 10″ piece

On a trip to a Chicago-area guild about twenty years ago, I was able to spend time with my aunt and uncle who lived in the area. They asked to see my quilts, and we ended up talking about how quilts are historical artifacts and can tell stories about the past. Having grown up during the Depression, my Aunt Jinny never put much stock in old things, always preferring new.

At the end of this discussion, Aunt Jinny turned to my Uncle Reed and suggested he bring up his "old blanket" from the basement. After unfolding the "old blanket" pulled from its sea chest, I gasped: I was looking at a perfectly preserved red-and-white Album block quilt complete with 42 signatures dated from 1841 to 1842. The signatures were from my Uncle Reed's Clayton ancestors, one of the founding families of the state of Delaware. The signatures were from 2 generations of the Clayton family, including men who had held the offices of United States Attorney General, Senator, and Governor of Delaware, along with other notable historic figures. Aunt Jinny was stunned at the importance of the quilt laid out in front of her. Uncle Reed was thoroughly pleased that his "old blanket" was just a bit more than that.

That historic quilt is now part of the textile archives of the Winterthur Museum, Garden & Library in Delaware.

CUTTING

Prepare a template from pattern O (pullout page P1).

Note: If you have an Omnigrip On Point Ruler, you can rotary cut the squares using the 2″ mark on the ruler in place of preparing Template O.

RED

◆ Cut 8 using Template O.

PINK

◆ Cut 4 using Template O.

CREAM

◆ Cut 1 using Template O.

◆ Cut 2 squares 3¼″ × 3¼″. Cut twice on the diagonal.

◆ Cut 2 squares 1⅞″ × 1⅞″. Cut once on the diagonal.

FRAMING STRIPS

◆ **Light green:** Use 4 strips 2″ × 8½″ from those already cut if you are making *The Anniversary Sampler Quilt* (page 19). For any of the other quilts, please see their specific cutting instructions.

MAKE THE BLOCK

Seam allowances are ¼″ unless otherwise noted. Press all seams in the direction of the arrows indicated in the diagrams.

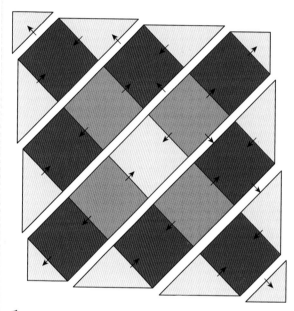

1. Sew assorted red and pink squares alternately with cream square, 8 quarter-square triangles, and 4 corner half-square triangles. Sew into rows. Join the rows.

2. Frame the block with 4 light green strips. Trim the block to 8½″ × 8½″. See Framing the Blocks (page 96).

Block 20: Single Irish Chain

The first full-fledged block exchange I participated in was some time ago with two friends from work. I was moving overseas, and our block exchange was a means to stay in touch with each other. We chose a variation of the Double Irish Chain for our quilts. Every three months we made three of the same block, kept one for ourselves, and exchanged the others, including a letter. Anticipating each new arrival was like waiting for Christmas packages.

Worn from use, I still have that quilt sitting on a rocking chair. It's soft and cuddly and just perfect for wrapping around small people for a delightful story time.

Chain blocks are attention grabbing because they visually draw the eye across the quilt. They can be quite elaborate or very simple, like this single chain, but their charm is in the simplicity of their construction and the variety of ways you can color them.

MATERIALS

 Red print: 4″ × 6″ piece

 Pink print: 4″ × 6″ piece

Cream solid: 10″ × 10″ square

CUTTING

RED

◆ Cut 6 squares 1½″ × 1½″.

PINK

◆ Cut 6 squares 1½″ × 1½″.

CREAM

◆ Cut 8 squares 1½″ × 1½″.

◆ Cut 4 squares 2½″ × 2½″.

FRAMING STRIPS

◆ **Light green:** Use 4 strips 2″ × 8½″ from those already cut if you are making *The Anniversary Sampler Quilt* (page 19). For any of the other quilts, please see their specific cutting instructions.

MAKE THE BLOCK

Seam allowances are ¼″ unless otherwise noted. Press all seams in the direction of the arrows indicated in the diagrams.

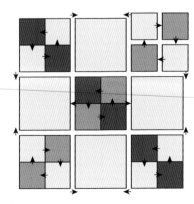

1. Sew together assorted red, pink, and cream squares.

2. Frame the block with 4 light green strips. Trim the block to 8½″ × 8½″. See Framing the Blocks (page 96).

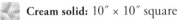

The Places Love Has Taken Me

You truly never know where life is going to take you or what's around the next corner. One year in late fall, while stationed in Germany, we packed up the family and headed to Berlin, where I had been invited to teach a workshop. Who could have predicted the fall of the Berlin Wall the week before my trip? But fall it did! Quilting placed us smack dab in the middle of one of history's most important events at the close of the twentieth century.

The wall was still up, but enough had been chopped away that people slipped through to the other side despite it still being heavily guarded. We weren't supposed to cross over, but the East German guards on the other side were as excited as us, grinning big and waving us over to get their pictures taken with those of us from the west. It was amazing. We still have our tote bag filled with chunks we chopped from the wall and memories of a lifetime.

You just never know. . . .

Small pieces of the Berlin wall along with my miniature North Carolina Lily quilt made on the way

Block 21: North Carolina Lily

MATERIALS

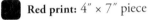 **Red print:** 4″ × 7″ piece

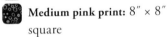 **Medium pink print:** 8″ × 8″ square

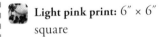 **Light pink print:** 6″ × 6″ square

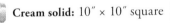 **Cream solid:** 10″ × 10″ square

Some of the earliest quilts I remember dreaming over were beautiful red-and-green North Carolina lily quilts. One fall, while working on a miniature version, my family joined me on a trip to Berlin. Even though the Berlin wall had just come down, the military checkpoints were not yet closed.

Before heading across into East Germany, there was a checkpoint where the service member had to go into a hut to get his paperwork approved and stamped before being allowed to continue. Family members had to stay in the car, and we were briefed beforehand to keep the windows rolled up and to make no eye contact or speak to the East German soldiers keeping an eye on us.

Our boys were preoccupied with their brand-new Game-boys in the back seat and probably don't remember that we sat there for an hour and a half, in the rain, waiting for and wondering if my husband was ever coming back. All the while, the soldiers circled the car, taking note of my sewing machine and equipment in the back of the station wagon. I was a wreck but kept my head down, working on appliqué-ing the border of my mini lily quilt.

When we finally made it to West Berlin, I took a look at my work and just about cried. I'd been so stressed that the appliqué border was pulled into a tight and puckered mess and it all had to come out. Anytime I pull out my little quilt, the memory of that nerve-wracking hour-and-a-half wait comes flooding back!

CUTTING

Prepare a template from pattern P (pullout page P1).

RED

- Cut 3 squares 2″ × 2″.

- Cut 1 piece ¾″ × 6″.

- Cut 2 pieces ¾″ × 1½″.

MEDIUM PINK

- Cut 2 squares 3⅜″ × 3⅜″. Cut once on the diagonal. You will have 1 leftover triangle if you are making 1 block.

- Cut 2 using Template P.

LIGHT PINK

- Cut 2 squares 2½″ × 2½″. Cut twice on the diagonal. You will have 2 leftover triangles if you are making 1 block.

CREAM

- Cut 1 square 4″ × 4″.

- Cut 2 squares 2½″ × 2½″. Cut twice on the diagonal. You will have 2 leftover triangles if you are making 1 block.

- Cut 3 squares 1¾″ × 1¾″.

- Cut 2 rectangles 1½″ × 3″.

FRAMING STRIPS

- **Light green:** Use 4 strips 2″ × 8½″ from those already cut if you are making *The Anniversary Sampler Quilt* (page 19). For any of the other quilts, please see their specific cutting instructions.

MAKE THE BLOCK

Seam allowances are ¼″ unless otherwise noted. Press all seams in the direction of the arrows indicated in the diagrams.

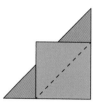

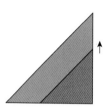

1. Draw a diagonal line on wrong side of red 2″ × 2″ squares. Sew them to corners of pink 3⅜″ half-square triangles. Make 3. See Folded Corners (page 10).

2. Sew together light pink and cream 2½″ quarter-square triangles. Half are a mirror image of the others. Make 3 of each. Sew 1 of each to sides of cream 1¾″ × 1¾″ square.

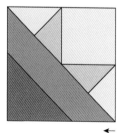

3. Sew together Step 1 and 2 units. Make 3 lilies.

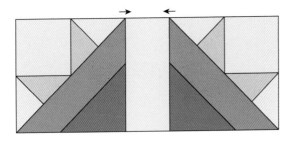

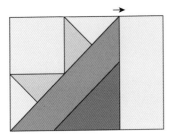

4. Sew 2 lilies to sides of 1 cream rectangle. Sew 1 cream rectangle to side of a third lily.

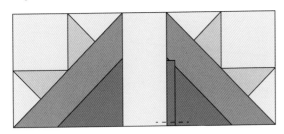

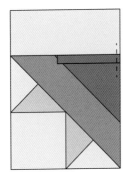

5. Turn under ¼" on both edges of long and short red stems. Place a short stem, right sides together, on the corners of 2 lilies, as shown. Nestle stems against seam ridge. Baste in place inside ¼" seamline. Baste long stem across diagonal of cream square, leaving excess tails past corners.

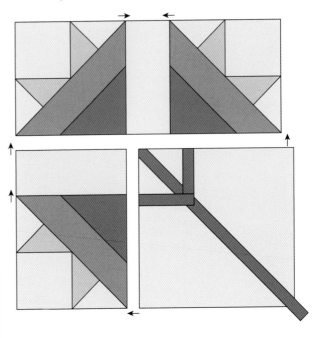

6. Sew together block parts. Stems will be attached at seams but loose. Unbaste part of long stem and flip short stems under long stem. Pin. Appliqué all stems in place. Turn under ¼" on leaves. Appliqué them in place.

7. Frame the block with 4 light green strips. Trim the block to 8½" × 8½". See Framing the Blocks (page 96).

Block 22: Kansas Winds

When we first moved to Kansas, everyone teased us about the tornadoes, winds, Dorothy, Toto, flying monkeys, and magic ruby slippers. There's a wonderful Wizard of Oz museum in Wamego, Kansas, but other than that we found no signs of Dorothy and company.

But the wind, now that's a whole 'nother story! Wind of some sort is the norm. And it whistles audibly around the roof of the house even at "low" speeds if your roof sits just right in relation to the prevailing winds. While most people like nice calm weather, Kansas weather never ceases to amaze and surprise me with its variety.

MATERIALS

 Red print: 5″ × 5″ square

 Pink print: 5″ × 10″ piece

 Cream solid: 5″ × 9″ piece

CUTTING

RED

◆ Cut 4 strips 1¼″ × 2″.

PINK

◆ Cut 4 strips 1¼″ × 2″.

◆ Cut 4 squares 2″ × 2″.

CREAM

◆ Cut 4 rectangles 2″ × 3½″.

FRAMING STRIPS

◆ **Light green:** Use 4 strips 2″ × 8½″ from those already cut if you are making *The Anniversary Sampler Quilt* (page 19). For any of the other quilts, please see their specific cutting instructions.

MAKE THE BLOCK

Seam allowances are ¼″ unless otherwise noted. Press all seams in the direction of the arrows indicated in the diagrams.

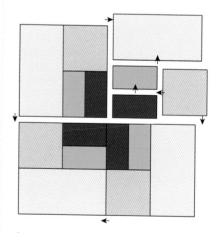

1. Sew together pink strips, red strips, pink squares, and cream rectangles.

2. Frame the block with 4 light green strips. Trim the block to 8½″ × 8½″. See Framing the Blocks (page 96).

Block 23: A Flock of Birds

A Flock of Birds composed of four single Birds in the Air blocks

On one of our tours in Germany, I had the opportunity to teach in a German quilt shop for quite a few years, as well as to the guilds forming throughout the country. I had mastered French in school and taken college-level German language courses during our previous tour. Since Frankfurt was an international community, those language skills gave me quite an advantage, as there was rarely a common language in my classes—I taught in all three.

Through my teaching I met a few French and German women who started a small bi-weekly get together at each other's homes and invited me to join the group. One day Marie-Therese brought one of her daughter's outgrown cotton pinafores and tore it up into pieces to share with each of us. What a treasure. The pretty blue print found its way into my *Birds in the Air* quilt, where it will always remind me of my wonderful friends and experiences across the ocean.

MATERIALS

 Assorted red prints: 4 pieces, each 5″ × 9″

 Cream solid: 7″ × 9″ piece

CUTTING

ASSORTED REDS

◆ Cut 2 squares 2″ × 2″ from each of the red prints. Cut each once on the diagonal. You will have 1 triangle left over from each print if you are making 1 block.

◆ Cut 1 square 3⅞″ × 3⅞″ from each of the 4 red prints. Cut each once on the diagonal. You will have 1 triangle left over from each print if you are making 1 block.

CREAM

Sort and label your 2″ and 1⅞″ cream triangles by size to avoid using them in the wrong place.

◆ Cut 6 squares 2″ × 2″. Cut once on the diagonal.

◆ Cut 6 squares 1⅞″ × 1⅞″. Cut once on the diagonal.

FRAMING STRIPS

◆ **Light green:** Use 4 strips 2″ × 8½″ from those already cut if you are making *The Anniversary Sampler Quilt* (page 19). For any of the other quilts, please see their specific cutting instructions.

MAKE THE BLOCK

Seam allowances are ¼″ unless otherwise noted. Press all seams in the direction of the arrows indicated in the diagrams.

Make 2.   Make 1.

1. Work with 1 red print at a time. Using the first red print, refer to Oversized Half-Square Triangle Units (page 9) to sew together 3 red and 3 cream 2″ triangles. Make 3 half-square triangle units. Follow the pressing directions carefully. Trim to 1½″.

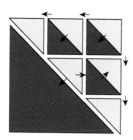

2. Sew together matching 3⅞″ red triangle, 3 cream 1⅞″ triangles, and half-square triangle units. Repeat for other 3 red prints.

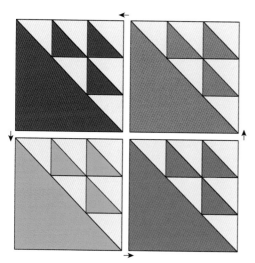

3. Sew together 4 Birds in the Air blocks.

4. Frame the block with 4 light green strips. Trim the block to 8½″ × 8½″. See Framing the Blocks (page 96).

Block 24: Outward Bound

Can you think of a better block to represent the lifestyle of a family always on the move? We had very few moves or trips without some sort of disaster or odd story, and it got to the point where we just laughed and added the stories to our growing list of "Thomas Family Travel Adventures."

There's the "hazmat move," with disasters on several different levels, the "plumber's nightmare" move, the "they lost Donna" trip, the "no more appliances" move, the "falling through the ceiling" event, and on and on. Outward bound and here comes the moving van.... Wagons, ho!

MATERIALS

 Red print: 6″ × 10″ piece

 Medium pink print: 6″ × 7″ square

Light pink print: 4″ × 7″ piece

Cream solid: 8″ × 8″ square

CUTTING

RED

◆ Cut 8 squares 1½″ × 1½″.

◆ Cut 1 square 2½″ × 2½″.

MEDIUM PINK

◆ Cut 8 rectangles 1½″ × 2½″.

LIGHT PINK

◆ Cut 8 squares 1½″ × 1½″.

CREAM

◆ Cut 16 squares 1½″ × 1½″.

FRAMING STRIPS

◆ **Light green:** Use 4 strips 2″ × 8½″ from those already cut if you are making *The Anniversary Sampler Quilt* (page 19). For any of the other quilts, please see their specific cutting instructions.

MAKE THE BLOCK

Seam allowances are ¼″ unless otherwise noted. Press all seams in the direction of the arrows indicated in the diagrams.

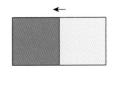

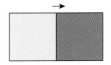

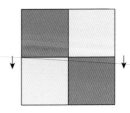

1. Sew together 2 cream and 2 red 1½″ × 1½″ squares. Make 4 four-patch units. Press exactly as directed so seams will nest later.

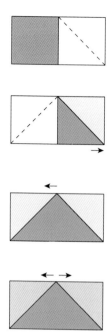

2. Draw a diagonal line on wrong side of 8 cream and 8 light pink 1½″ × 1½″ squares. Sew cream squares to corners of medium pink rectangles. Make 4 Flying Geese units. Make 4 more Flying Geese with light pink corners. See Folded Corners (page 10).

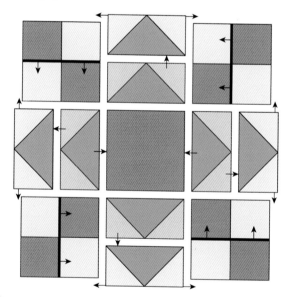

3. Sew together Flying Geese, four-patch units, and red center square. Carefully orient the long final seam of four-patches, as shown by dark lines in diagram. If not, some four-patch seams won't nest with the Flying Geese units.

4. Frame the block with 4 light green strips. Trim the block to 8½″ × 8½″. See Framing the Blocks (page 96).

A Piece of My Heart

As an infantry soldier, my husband spent many, many months each year out on field training exercises, especially during our tours to Germany. This was in the days before cell phones, so there was no contact other than an occasional letter. His absence meant I wore all the hats and made all decisions in the family, trying to juggle scouts, sports, and school activities along with the myriad of volunteer and unit activities required of military spouses in those days.

Meanwhile, the friendship of my German and French patchwerk group helped to keep me grounded, providing a sense of normality outside of the demands of Army life. We'd meet every other week and talk about our children, families, and quilting projects over delicious kaffee and kuchen. Quilting was my source of balance and comfort, as it has been for so many women over the generations.

Inscription on the hearts: *Dearest Terry, Here is my heart. Carry it with you always for you are the missing piece. Only you can return it whole. —Donna*

Block 25: A Piece of My Heart

He returned, and so our hearts are whole again in this rendition of my *Desert Storm Hearts*.

Desert Storm brought a new element to our military way of life. My husband, Terry, was assigned to the Third Armored Division and deployed to the Middle East from Germany. We didn't know where or what Terry would be doing during the war, how long it would last, or when he'd return. All I knew was that a piece of my heart would go with him, leaving a hole in what was left.

I made a patchwork heart with a hole in the center for each of us to wear for the duration. It's a quilter's heart, a soldier's wife's heart. He brought it home six months later, filling that hole, and I am forever grateful.

Not all of our soldiers made it home. The memory of one young captain, his wife, and their two children will be with me all my days. Thinking about reading the grieving widow her husband's last "just in case ... " letter leaves me sobbing to this day. He is not forgotten, though, as he lives on in my memories.

MATERIALS

 Assorted red prints: 7 squares, each 3″ × 3″ *or* assorted scraps

 Cream solid: 1 square 8″ × 8″

CUTTING

Prepare a template from pattern Q (pullout page P1).

ASSORTED REDS

◆ Cut a total of 25 squares, each 1½″ × 1½″.

CREAM

◆ Cut 1 square 6½″ × 6½″.

FRAMING STRIPS

◆ **Medium green:** Use 4 strips 2″ × 8½″ from those already cut if you are making *The Anniversary Sampler Quilt* (page 19). For any of the other quilts, please see their specific cutting instructions.

MAKE THE BLOCK

Seam allowances are ¼″ unless otherwise noted. Press all seams in the direction of the arrows indicated in the diagrams.

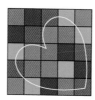

1. Sew 25 red squares into 5 rows of 5 blocks. Press. Use Template Q to cut a heart from pieced patch.

Note: Template Q does not include turn-under seam allowances. If your preferred method of appliqué preparation requires a turn-under seam allowance, please add it when cutting out your heart.

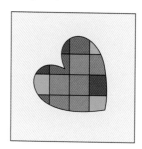

2. Prepare, center, and appliqué heart diagonally on the 6½″ × 6½″ cream square.

3. Frame the block with 4 medium green strips. Trim the block to 8½″ × 8½″. See Framing the Blocks (page 96).

Block 26: Cupid's Arrow

Cupid shot a big old arrow through my heart with the birth of each of my granddaughters. I had no clue just how special and wonderful the bond with these new little people could be until they were born. Like so many experiences, the deep and special love between grandparents and grandchildren is a feeling you can't imagine until it happens.

I have a quilt full of pink-and-green Cupid's Arrow blocks that waits for my granddaughters' visits.

MATERIALS

 Assorted red prints: 4 squares, each 5″ × 5″

 Assorted pink prints: 4 squares, each 3″ × 3″

 Cream solid: 1 square 9″ × 9″

CUTTING

ASSORTED REDS

◆ Cut 2 rectangles 2″ × 3½″ from each of the 4 prints.

ASSORTED PINKS

◆ Cut 1 square 2″ × 2″ from each of the 4 prints.

CREAM

◆ Cut 12 squares 2″ × 2″.

FRAMING STRIPS

◆ **Light green:** Use 4 strips 2″ × 8½″ from those already cut if you are making *The Anniversary Sampler Quilt* (page 19). For any of the other quilts, please see their specific cutting instructions.

MAKE THE BLOCK

Seam allowances are ¼″ unless otherwise noted. Press all seams in the direction of the arrows indicated in the diagrams.

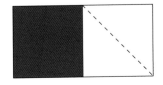

1. Draw a diagonal line on wrong side of pink and cream squares. Sew a cream square on opposite sides of a red rectangle. Repeat with a rectangle of each red print. See Folded Corners (page 10).

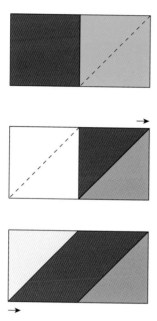

2. In the same fashion as Step 1, make 4 more rectangle units, using 1 pink and 1 cream corner for each. Be careful because the 2 types of rectangles are mirror images of each other. Press the seams in the directions indicated.

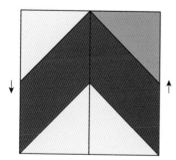

3. Sew the like-colored rectangle units into pairs to make 4 chevrons. Press the center seam to the right on 2 pairs and to the left on the other 2 pairs.

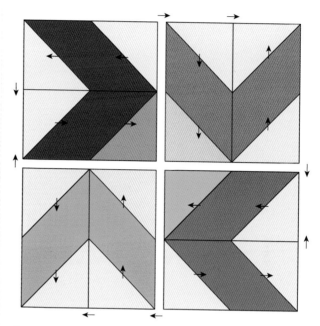

4. Arrange the blocks so that the seams nest as shown. Sew together chevrons.

5. Frame the block with 4 light green strips. Trim the block to 8½″ × 8½″. See Framing the Blocks (page 96).

Block 27: Memory

Our lives are our memories acquired through time. Some make you chuckle, and others leave you howling with laughter no matter how many years later. Some are sad, some fade, and others are so crystal clear that time is distorted and folded back on itself. My oldest son is grown, married, and has children of his own. His hair is graying, yet in him I still see the adorable baby he was and every age in between.

I especially cherish one night spent in a rocking chair with his warm breath and little face buried in my neck. Not wanting to put him back in his crib, I sensed that a lifelong memory was in the making. That sweet night is as fresh in my mind as it was 38 years ago and will continue to warm my heart until I take my last breath.

MATERIALS

 Red print: 9″ × 9″ square

 Medium pink print: 7″ × 6″ square

 Light pink print: 4″ × 4″ square

 Cream solid: 6″ × 10″ piece

CUTTING

RED

◆ Cut 8 squares 1½″ × 1½″.

◆ Cut 1 square 2½″ × 2½″.

◆ Cut 4 squares 2″ × 2″. Cut each once on the diagonal.

MEDIUM PINK

◆ Cut 8 rectangles 1½″ × 2½″.

LIGHT PINK

◆ Cut 4 squares 1½″ × 1½″.

CREAM

◆ Cut 12 squares 1½″ × 1½″.

◆ Cut 4 squares 2″ × 2″. Cut each once on the diagonal.

FRAMING STRIPS

◆ **Medium green:** Use 4 strips 2″ × 8½″ from those already cut if you are making *The Anniversary Sampler Quilt* (page 19). For any of the other quilts, please see their specific cutting instructions.

MAKE THE BLOCK

Seam allowances are ¼″ unless otherwise noted. Press all seams in the direction of the arrows indicated in the diagrams.

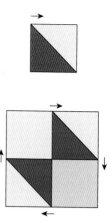

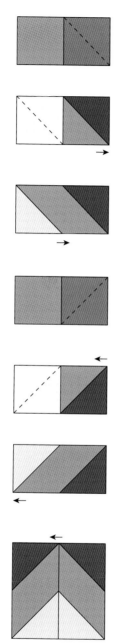

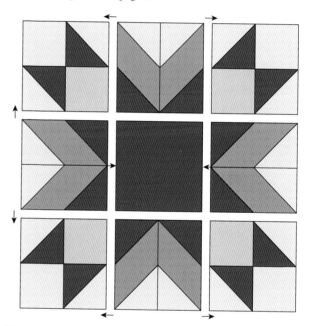

1. Draw a diagonal line on wrong side of 8 red and 8 cream 1½″ × 1½″ squares.

Make 4 of each rectangle unit. Be careful because 4 of the rectangle units must be mirror images of the other 4. Sew rectangle units into pairs. Make 4 chevrons. See Folded Corners (page 10).

2. Sew dark red half-square triangles to cream half-square triangles. Press. Trim to 1½″. Make 8. Sew together half square triangle units, cream 1½″ × 1½″ squares, and light pink 1½″ × 1½″ squares. Make 4 corner units. See Oversized Half-Square Triangle Units (page 9).

3. Sew together chevrons, red 2½″ × 2½″ square, and corner units.

4. Frame the block with 4 medium green strips. Trim the block to 8½″ × 8½″. See Framing the Blocks (page 96).

Block 28: Capital T

The focus in my life is family—the four Thomases. As time marches forward, our family grows and becomes richer. Now, numbering more than the four T's in one block, we've added Katie, Charlotte, and Alexandra, and, in the not-too-distant future, a new daughter-in-law will grace our family. With luck, someday I'll need to make a big quilt full of Capital T blocks to account for them all.

MATERIALS

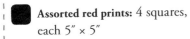Assorted red prints: 4 squares, each 5″ × 5″

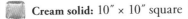Cream solid: 10″ × 10″ square

CUTTING

ASSORTED REDS

◆ Cut 1 square 3″ × 3″ from each of the 4 red prints. Cut each once on the diagonal. You will have 1 leftover triangle from each print if you are making 1 block.

◆ Cut 5 squares 1½″ × 1½″ from each of the 4 red prints.

CREAM

◆ Cut 2 squares 3″ × 3″. Cut each once on the diagonal.

◆ Cut 1 square 2½″ × 2½″.

◆ Cut 8 rectangles 1½″ × 2½″.

FRAMING STRIPS

◆ Medium green: Use 4 strips 2″ × 8½″ from those already cut if you are making *The Anniversary Sampler Quilt* (page 19). For any of the other quilts, please see their cutting instructions.

MAKE THE BLOCK

Seam allowances are ¼" unless otherwise noted. Press all seams in the direction of the arrows indicated in the diagrams.

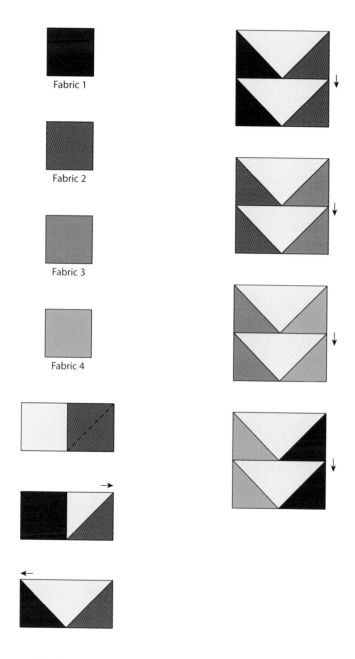

1. Assign each red print a number from 1 to 4. Make 2 of each type of rectangle unit shown. Pay careful attention to print number placement. Sew rectangles into pairs. Make 4 Flying Geese units. See Folded Corners (page 10).

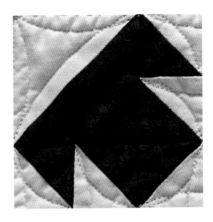

2. Make block center using 4 remaining red 2″ × 2″ squares and large cream 2½″ × 2½″ square. Pay careful attention to print placement.

3. Referring to Oversized Half-Square Triangle Units (page 9), sew a large red half-square triangle to a cream half-square triangle. Press. Trim to 2½″.

4. Sew together block center, half-square triangle units, and Flying Geese units. Carefully place pieces so same red prints sit next to each other.

5. Frame the block with the 4 medium green strips. Trim the block to 8½″ × 8½″. See Framing the Blocks (page 96).

The Threads of Life

Anyone who has lived long enough knows that life isn't always sunshine and roses. Along with periods of joy and wonder, there are tough times, sad times, and times that see you holding onto a day one hour at a time. We find our way through, but I think we quilters have something special to help us. Our threads and needles see us through those tough times, keeping our hands busy and our hearts focused on the things that matter.

Mother's Stars in Heaven by Donna Lynn Thomas, 63″ × 63″

Close-up of a mirrored star block

Block 29: LeMoyne Star

MATERIALS

Note: Gather materials for either option 1 (mirrored stars) or option 2 (plain stars using 2 prints).

 Cream solid: 1 square 10″ × 10″

Option 1: Mirrored stars

 Red print: ¼–½ yard of symmetrical repeat *or* enough fabric to be able to cut 8 repeats of any motif you choose

Option 2: Plain stars

 Red print: 5″ × 8″ piece

 Pink print: 5″ × 8″ piece

My mother was of the generation that smoked. She eventually quit, but not before it had taken its toll. Retired from the Army, we settled near her home to help. During her last nine years, she spent a good bit of time in and out of ICU and the hospital while we sat vigil by her side for hours on end. Throughout those years, I hand pieced dozens of LeMoyne stars. Each diamond was fussy cut from border prints or symmetrical repeat prints using mirrors to determine my design. Piecing kept my hands busy, freeing my mind to focus on my mother and her needs.

Beyond my own concerns, my hand piecing started conversations and relationships with other families waiting for their loved ones, taking our minds off our own troubles for bits of time. We grew to know the nursing staff, celebrating their weddings, births, and anniversaries as they occurred over those years as we sat with my mother. And my stack of blocks grew.

After my mother passed away, I made a quilt in her memory using 25 of the mirrored stars. Periodically, I find a beautiful new piece of fabric to cut and sew into more stars to add to my collection, all the while remembering those bittersweet threads of life that saw me through some pretty rough years.

Mirrored Stars

Although I fussy cut my diamonds using mirrors, you don't need to do so. You can choose option 2 and make your star using one red print and one pink print. If you do wish to give mirrored stars a try, follow these steps:

1. Using Template R to find the correct angle, place a pair of hinged mirrors on any interesting position of a symmetrical repeat print. The effect of the final star will be seen in the mirrors. Keep moving the mirror position until you find the effect you like.

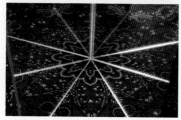

2. Using a fine-line chalk marker, place finished-size Template R on the repeat you chose and trace around it. Find and mark 7 more of the exact same repeats for a total of 8.

3. Pin-mark the points of the repeat. On the reverse side, align the template points with the pins and draw the sewing line. Cut out the diamonds ¼″ from the marked line.

CUTTING

Prepare a template from pattern R (pullout page P1).

Note: Follow cutting instructions based on either option 1 (mirrored stars) or 2 (plain stars using 2 prints).

CREAM

- Cut 4 squares 2¼″ × 2¼″.
- Cut 1 square 3¼″ × 3¼″. Cut twice on the diagonal.

OPTION 1: MIRRORED STARS

Red repeat

- Cut 8 using Template R.

OPTION 2: PLAIN STARS

Red

- Cut 4 using Template R.

Pink

- Cut 4 using Template R.

FRAMING STRIPS

- **Light green:** Use 4 strips 2″ × 8½″ from those already cut if you are making *The Anniversary Sampler Quilt* (page 19). For any of the other quilts, please see their specific cutting instructions.

MAKE THE BLOCK

Seam allowances are ¼″ unless otherwise noted. Press all seams in the direction of the arrows indicated in the diagrams.

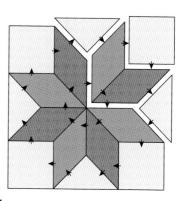

1. Sew together 8 diamonds. For fussy-cut diamonds, pin mark several matching points along the sewing line so the repeat is continuous. Set in cream pieces.

2. Frame the block with the 4 light green strips. Trim the block to 8½″ × 8½″. See Framing the Blocks (page 96).

Block 30: Ann's Pinwheel

Several years ago, I was designing and writing patterns for a new book. I was on the phone one night with Ann, a friend of many years, who had a newly finished wall-hanging that was perfect for the book. Among other things, we talked that night about all the projects she had contributed to or quilted for my books over the years.

The next morning, a mutual friend called to tell me Ann had passed away in her sleep the night before without any warning whatsoever. She wasn't even 50 years old. Tears still come to my eyes at the too-young loss of such a good friend. The original name for this block is forgotten. It will always be Ann's Pinwheel to me. Quilters have always done that, haven't we? We name blocks for events and people that mean something to us.

MATERIALS

 Red print: 5″ × 8″ piece

 Pink print: 5″ × 9″ piece

Cream solid: 6″ × 6″ piece

CUTTING

Prepare a template from pattern R (pullout page P1).

RED

◆ Cut 4 using Template R.

PINK

◆ Cut 2 squares 3⅞″ × 3⅞″. Cut each once on the diagonal.

CREAM

◆ Cut 2 squares 2⅛″ × 2⅛″. Cut each once on the diagonal.

◆ Cut 2 squares 2⅝″ × 2⅝″. Cut each once on the diagonal.

FRAMING STRIPS

◆ **Light green:** Use 4 strips 2″ × 8½″ from those already cut if you are making *The Anniversary Sampler Quilt* (page 19). For any of the other quilts, please see their specific cutting instructions.

MAKE THE BLOCK

Seam allowances are ¼″ unless otherwise noted. Press all seams in the direction of the arrows indicated in the diagrams.

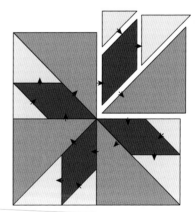

1. Sew 2 cream triangles to sides of a red diamond. Make 4. Pay close attention to which triangle goes on which side. Sew diamond units to large pink triangles. Sew together quarter-blocks.

2. Frame the block with the 4 light green strips. Trim the block to 8½″ × 8½″. See Framing the Blocks (page 96).

Block 31: My Three Vets

Sounds like that old TV show, *My Three Sons*, doesn't it? (But my husband and I have just two sons, not three.) Military service seems to run in our family. Along with my husband and both my sons, my father and father-in-law served. My husband and two sons all saw combat, so I designed this block a few years ago to honor the three most important men in my life—my three vets!

MATERIALS

 Red print: 7″ × 9″ piece

 Pink print: 8″ × 8″ square

 Cream solid: 8″ × 10″ piece

CUTTING

RED

◆ Cut 12 squares 2″ × 2″.

PINK

◆ Cut 4 rectangles 2″ × 2½″.

◆ Cut 1 square 3½″ × 3½″.

CREAM

◆ Cut 8 rectangles 2″ × 3¼″.

FRAMING STRIPS

◆ **Medium green:** Use 4 strips 2″ × 8½″ from those already cut if you are making *The Anniversary Sampler Quilt* (page 19). For any of the other quilts, please see their specific cutting instructions.

MAKE THE BLOCK

Seam allowances are ¼″ unless otherwise noted. Press all seams in the direction of the arrows indicated in the diagrams.

1. Draw a diagonal line on wrong side of each red square. Sew red square to corner of cream rectangle. Make 4. Press. See Folded Corners (page 10).

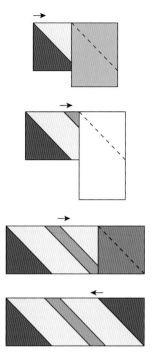

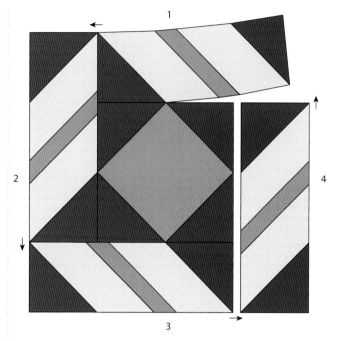

2. Draw a 45° angle line on remaining cream and pink rectangles. Make 4 striped rectangles using cream rectangles, pink rectangles, red squares, and units from Step 1. See Striped Units (page 11).

3. Draw diagonal line on wrong side of 4 red squares. Sew them to corners of 3½″ × 3½″ pink square.

4. Sew striped rectangles to center unit using partial seams (page 18).

5. Frame the block with the 4 medium green strips. Trim the block to 8½″ × 8½″. See Framing the Blocks (page 96).

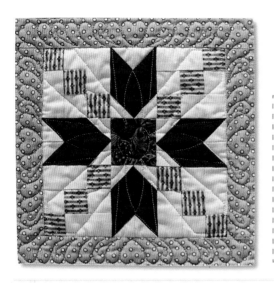

MATERIALS

Very dark red print: 3″ × 3″ piece

Red print: 4″ × 6″ piece

 Pink print: 6″ × 6″ square

Cream solid: 10″ × 10″ square

Some people enter your life in unanticipated ways. Such is the case with BJ and Sabra Fleming. My father and BJ served in the Army together and became fast and dear friends. They met as young civil engineers learning to fly both helicopters and fixed-wing aircraft for the Army Air Corps. They moved from school to school around the country, eventually landing at the Presidio in San Francisco.

BJ flew the first Otters from the manufacturer to San Francisco in early 1955. Then in April of that year, my father flew one of them to Alaska while BJ headed north by ship. As a result of the developing Cold War, they were on the way to their assignment to survey and create topographical maps of Alaska in preparation for the installation of the Distant Early Warning Lines (DEW Lines) in northern Alaska. Aside from that, the arrival of those first Otters became quite an historic event for Alaska as well, opening up the bush country when the Army sold their Otters to private pilots.

Once there, my father traded the Otter for the small helicopter he would use to survey and run supplies from site to site. My mother, nearing the end of her pregnancy, anxiously waited at home in Pennsylvania with her parents for my father's return at the end of the summer. Late in June, on a return flight from Pt. Barrow, an Arctic owl flew into his tail rotor. He crashed, and though rescued and pulled from the wreckage, he died 3 days later in Alaska at the young age of 26. I was born 4 days later. He returned home, but not as my mother had longed for. He was buried in Pennsylvania in early July of 1955.

BJ and Sabra have kept in touch with me all my life, writing and remembering me for every event large and small, but I didn't meet them in person until 28 years later. Since then, they've become like a second set of parents to me.

Growing up I always recognized their letters immediately, as they were addressed to Donna *Lynn*, a double name that only they used. When I married, I kept my middle name in their honor and have used it professionally ever since. The Flemings have been steppingstones to a father I never met but knew very well through the stories of their times together. But more than that, their love and devotion through all these years has meant the world to me.

CUTTING

VERY DARK RED

◆ Cut 1 square 2″ × 2″.

RED

◆ Cut 8 rectangles 1¼″ × 2¾″.

PINK

◆ Cut 12 squares 1¼″ × 1¼″.

CREAM

◆ Cut 24 squares 1¼″ × 1¼″.

◆ Cut 8 rectangles 1¼″ × 2″.

FRAMING STRIPS

◆ **Light green:** Use 4 strips 2″ × 8½″ from those already cut if you're making *The Anniversary Sampler Quilt* (page 19). For any of the other quilts, please see their specific cutting instructions.

MAKE THE BLOCK

Seam allowances are ¼″ unless otherwise noted. Press all seams in the direction of the arrows indicated in the diagrams.

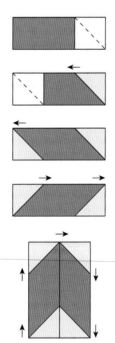

1. Draw a diagonal line on wrong side of 16 cream squares. Sew cream squares to corners of red rectangles. Press. Make 4 each of 2 types of rectangles shown. Be careful because 4 of the rectangle units must be mirror images of the other 4. Sew rectangles into pairs. Make 4 chevrons. See Folded Corners (page 10).

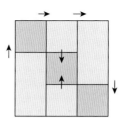

2. Sew together pink squares, cream squares, and rectangles.

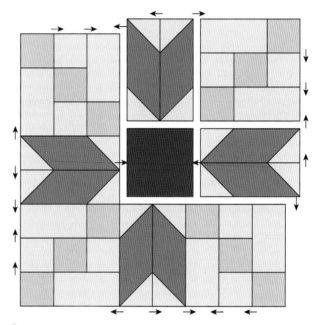

3. Sew together block corners, very dark red square, and chevrons.

4. Frame the block with the 4 light green strips and trim the block to 8½″ × 8½″. See Framing the Blocks (page 96).

It's Fun to Play

With quilt blocks, that is! Give me a piece of graph paper, a pencil, and a ruler, and I'll be entertained for hours playing and modifying existing blocks or creating new ones altogether. Of course I use quilt design software more often than not these days, but the idea is the same.

I was one of those annoying students who loved geometry and all those delightful proofs and theorems. I'd ask for more homework and never got my fill of the joy of figuring it all out. Just a tiny bit of a misogynist, my teacher wouldn't give me more homework because he said I was a girl and wouldn't need it! Can you imagine? I mailed him a copy of one of my books years ago with the inscription, "See? I did need it!"

Needless to say, logic puzzles and jigsaw puzzles are other passions of mine, right along with the geometry of playing with quilt blocks and figuring out new ways to do things.

So here are some of my favorite "adapted" quilt blocks.

Star Trails by Donna Lynn Thomas, 75½″ × 75½″

Star Trails is adapted from the simple Friendship Star block. It came to be by substituting striped rectangles and striped squares for the plain half-square triangles and corners.

Block 33: Sleight of Hand

One of the things I like to do is "stripe up" a block design. If you wander through Barbara Brackman's *Encyclopedia of Pieced Quilt Patterns*, you'll find a ton of interesting old blocks using striped units. Of course, the blocks would have been cut with templates. I figured out a way to do it with simple rotary-cut squares and rectangles, and started modifying existing blocks just because I could.

Adapting the old Card Tricks block, I substituted the original half-square and quarter-square triangles with striped squares and triangles to make this unique little variation.

MATERIALS

 Red print: 7" × 7" square

 Pink print: 7" × 7" square

Cream solid: 10" × 10" square

CUTTING

Label your triangles by size as you cut them to avoid confusion.

RED

- Cut 1 square 2½" × 2½".

- Cut 1 square 3" × 3". Cut once on the diagonal.

- Cut 1 square 2⅞" × 2⅞". Cut once on the diagonal.

- Cut 1 square 3¼" × 3¼". Cut twice on the diagonal. You will have 2 leftover triangles if you are making 1 block.

PINK

- Cut 1 square 3" × 3". Cut once on the diagonal.

- Cut 1 square 2⅞" × 2⅞". Cut once on the diagonal.

- Cut 1 square 3¼" × 3¼". Cut twice on the diagonal. You will have 2 leftover triangles if you are making 1 block.

CREAM

- Cut 2 squares 3" × 3". Cut each once on the diagonal.

- Cut 1 square 3¼" × 3¼". Cut twice on the diagonal.

- Cut 2 squares 2⅜" × 2⅜". Cut each once on the diagonal.

- Cut 8 squares 2" × 2".

FRAMING STRIPS

- **Medium green:** Use 4 strips 2" × 8½" from those already cut if you are making *The Anniversary Sampler Quilt* (page 19). For any of the other quilts, please see their specific cutting instructions.

MAKE THE BLOCK

Seam allowances are ¼″ unless otherwise noted. Press all seams in the direction of the arrows indicated in the diagrams.

1. Referring to Oversized Half-Square Triangle Units (page 9), sew 2 red and 2 pink 3″ triangles to 4 cream 3″ triangles. Make 4. Trim each to 2½″.

2. Draw a diagonal line on wrong side of 4 cream 2″ × 2″ squares. Sew them to colored corners of each unit from Step 1. Make 2 pink striped squares and 2 red striped squares. Press. Trim. See Folded Corners (page 10).

3. Draw a diagonal line on wrong side of 4 cream 2″ × 2″ squares. Sew them to colored corners of 2 red and 2 pink 2⅞″ half-square triangles. Press. Trim. See Folded Corners (page 10).

4. Sew a 3¼″ cream quarter-square triangle to 2 red and 2 pink 3¼″ quarter-square triangles. Press.

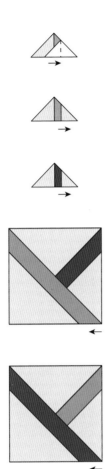

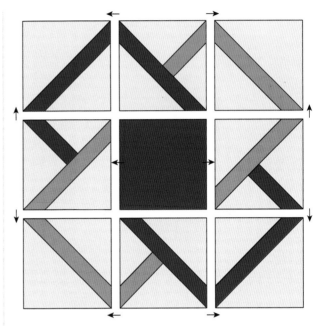

5. Draw a vertical line in center of cream 2⅜″ half-square triangles. Sew them to corner units from Step 4. Make 4. Trim. Sew each pink unit to red striped triangle from Step 3. Sew each red unit to pink striped triangle from Step 3. See Striped Units (page 11).

6. Arrange assorted block patches with dark red 2½″ × 2½″ square, as shown. Pay careful attention to color location and unit orientation. Sew the patches into rows, and sew together the rows to complete a block.

7. Frame the block with the 4 medium green strips. Trim the block to 8½″ × 8½″. See Framing the Blocks (page 96).

Block 34: Shimmering Leaf

Value is key to making this block work. Leaf blocks are simple to make, but I thought it would be interesting to make them shimmer, so I used striped rectangles in place of the original plain half-square triangle units. The stem is also made with a striped square.

The leaf shimmer is created not just through the stripes but more importantly through the value gradation of those stripes. Work with one color family and choose a dark, medium, and light print in that family. Try not to use high-contrast multicolor prints but rather more subtle prints.

Be careful—your friends with vertigo may not be able to look at a quilt full of shimmering leaves!

MATERIALS

 Dark red print: 5″ × 9″ piece

 Medium red print: 5″ × 9″ piece

 Pink print: 4″ × 7″ piece

 Cream solid: 8″ × 8″ square

CUTTING

DARK RED

- Cut 6 squares 2″ × 2″.
- Cut 1 rectangle 2″ × 3½″.

MEDIUM RED

- Cut 4 rectangles 2″ × 2¾″.
- 1 square 1½″ × 1½″.

PINK

- Cut 4 rectangles 2″ × 2¾″.
- Cut 1 strip 1″ × 1½″.
- Cut 1 strip 1″ × 2″.

CREAM

- Cut 5 squares 2″ × 2″.
- Cut 1 rectangle 2″ × 3½″.
- Cut 2 squares 1¾″ × 1¾″.

FRAMING STRIPS

- **Light green:** Use 4 strips 2″ × 8½″ from those already cut if you are making *The Anniversary Sampler Quilt* (page 19). For any of the other quilts, please see their specific cutting instructions.

MAKE THE BLOCK

Seam allowances are ¼″ unless otherwise noted. Press all seams in the direction of the arrows indicated in the diagrams.

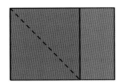

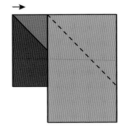

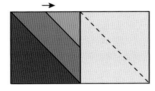

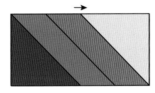

1. Draw a diagonal line on wrong side of 2 dark red squares. Sew dark red squares to corners of 2 medium red rectangles. Draw a 45° line on 2 pink 2″ × 3½″ rectangles and 2 cream squares. Make 2 striped rectangles. See Folded Corners (page 10) and Striped Units (page 11).

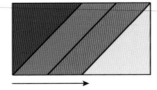

2. Repeat Step 1. Make 2 mirror-image striped rectangles.

3. Draw a diagonal line on wrong side of 2 cream 1¾″ × 1¾″ squares. Sew to opposite sides of dark red 2″ × 2″ square to make the stem. See Folded Corners (page 10).

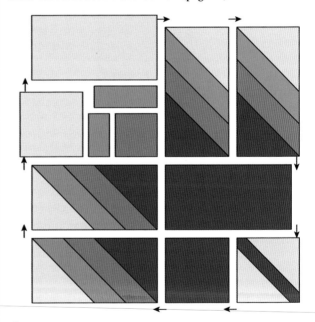

4. Sew together stem, striped rectangles, and remaining pieces.

5. Frame the block with the 4 light green strips. Trim the block to 8½″ × 8½″. See Framing the Blocks (page 96).

Block 35: Candy Dots

Similar to Jacob's Ladder, this block has a wonderful diagonal pull. Such blocks make for some exciting and creative quilt designs when they're set together straight without sashes and twisted and turned in different directions. Hello, design wall!

Wanting something interesting to happen on the plain corners when blocks are set straight together, I used the folded corner concept to come up with an easy way to make what look like tiny pieced triangles on the two opposite corners.

Once done, I added circles down the middle for a bit of whimsy. In the end, it reminded me of those papers stuck with multicolored candy dots that we used to buy at our local penny-candy stores.

MATERIALS

 Red print: 7″ × 7″ square

 Pink print: 6″ × 6″ square

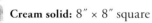 **Cream solid:** 8″ × 8″ square

CUTTING

Prepare a template from pattern S (pullout page P1).

RED

◆ Cut 2 squares 3″ × 3″. Cut each once on the diagonal.

◆ Cut 3 using Template S.

PINK

◆ Cut 3 squares 2½″ × 2½″.

◆ Cut 1 square 2″ × 2″. Cut once on the diagonal.

CREAM

◆ Cut 2 squares 3″ × 3″. Cut each once on the diagonal.

◆ Cut 2 squares 2½″ × 2½″.

◆ Cut 1 square 2″ × 2″. Cut once on the diagonal.

FRAMING STRIPS

◆ **Medium green:** Use 4 strips 2″ × 8½″ from those already cut if you are making *The Anniversary Sampler Quilt* (page 19). For any of the other quilts, please see their specific cutting instructions.

MAKE THE BLOCK

Seam allowances are ¼" unless otherwise noted. Press all seams in the direction of the arrows indicated in the diagrams.

Depending on your method of appliqué, use Template S either with or without seam allowances included.

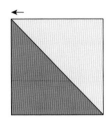

1. Referring to Oversized Half-Square Triangle Units (page 9), sew 4 red 3" triangles to 4 cream 3" triangles. Press. Trim to 2½". Sew 2 pink 2" triangles to 2 cream 2" triangles. Press. Trim to 1½".

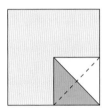

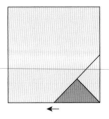

2. Draw a diagonal line on wrong side of 2 small pink-and-cream half-square triangle units. Sew each half-square triangle unit to corner of cream 2½" × 2½" square. See Folded Corners (page 10).

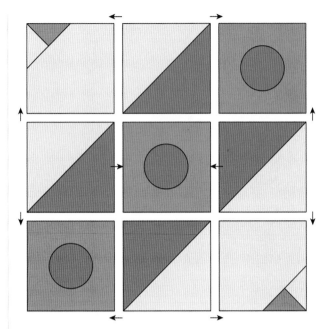

3. Sew together red/cream half-square triangles, pink 2½" × 2½" squares, and corner units from Step 2. Prepare and appliqué piece S circles to centers of pink squares.

4. Frame the block with the 4 medium green strips. Trim the block to 8½" × 8½". See Framing the Blocks (page 96).

Block 36: Shifting Winds

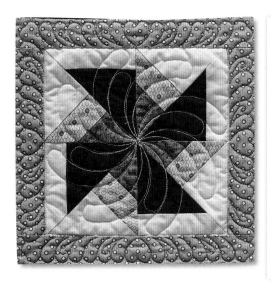

Windmill blocks come in all kinds of variations. Generally easy to make, they can be quite striking in design. The most complex Windmill blocks have stripes in the triangles. Simpler ones can be striped up in many ways. This is one of the earlier ones I "adapted," but there have been many more since. The appeal is in the spin. For the quilt made from this block, I alternated the direction of the spin from block to block, thus creating shifting winds.

MATERIALS

 Red print: 5″ × 9″ piece

 Medium pink print: 5″ × 9″ piece

 Light pink print: 4″ × 7″ piece

 Cream solid: 8″ × 8″ square

CUTTING

RED

◆ Cut 2 squares 3⅛″ × 3⅛″. Cut each once on the diagonal.

MEDIUM PINK

◆ Cut 2 squares 2¾″ × 2¾″. Cut each once on the diagonal.

LIGHT PINK

◆ Cut 1 square 4¼″ × 4¼″. Cut twice on the diagonal.

CREAM

◆ Cut 4 rectangles 1¼″ × 3½″.

◆ Cut 1 square 4¼″ × 4¼″. Cut twice on the diagonal.

FRAMING STRIPS

◆ **Light green:** Use 4 strips 2″ × 8½″ from those already cut if you are making *The Anniversary Sampler Quilt* (page 19). For any of the other quilts, please see their specific cutting instructions.

MAKE THE BLOCK

Seam allowances are ¼″ unless otherwise noted. Press all seams in the direction of the arrows indicated in the diagrams.

1. Sew red triangles to cream rectangles. Press. Trim excess cream rectangle tail even with long edge of red triangle.

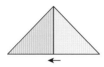

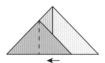

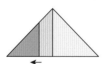

2. Sew together cream 4¼″ triangle and light pink 4¼″ triangle. Make 4. Draw a line on wrong side of a medium pink triangle. Sew it to corner of triangle unit. Press. Trim. See Striped Units (page 11).

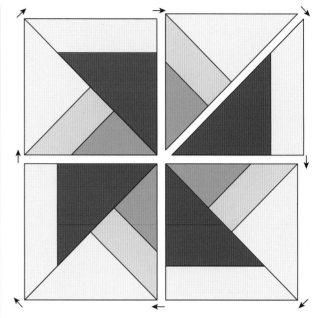

3. Sew together assorted units. Press.

4. Frame the block with the 4 light green strips. Trim the block to 8½″ × 8½″. See Framing the Blocks (page 96).

What Goes Around Comes Around

Do you ever find yourself using the same block over and over again because you like it so much? If I had to choose, the four in this chapter would be at the top of the list of my all-time favorites.

They've appeared in many of my books and classes as samples of different ideas. In some cases, I just like the way they look. As with so many things in life, there's a certain comfort in familiarity, and I think we quilters take that to our craft when we find favorite blocks.

When I'm not sure what else to do but want to sew, I turn to certain blocks or patterns because they're like old friends or comfortable slippers. I know I can sit down and make them almost without thinking, simply enjoying the process of creating without pressures or deadlines.

Eveningshades by Donna Lynn Thomas, 43½" × 43½"

Block 37: Folded Box

My husband teases me that not all blocks can be my favorite, but in this case it truly is! I love how you can create a three-dimensional look in the design simply through the use of value. The key is to choose one color family and then select a dark, medium, and light print within that color family along with a background print.

I've used Folded Box over and over again in full-size blocks, miniature ones, and everything in between. These colored boxes bedazzle me every time I make one.

MATERIALS

 Dark red print: 7″ × 7″ square

 Medium red print: 4″ × 7″ piece

 Pink print: 3″ × 7″ piece

 Cream solid: 7″ × 7″ square

CUTTING

DARK RED

◆ Cut 1 square 2½″ × 2½″.

◆ Cut 8 squares 1½″ × 1½″.

MEDIUM RED

◆ Cut 2 squares 3″ × 3″. Cut each once on the diagonal.

PINK

◆ Cut 4 rectangles 1½″ × 2½″.

CREAM

◆ Cut 2 squares 3″ × 3″. Cut each once on the diagonal.

◆ Cut 4 rectangles 1½″ × 2½″.

FRAMING STRIPS

◆ **Medium green:** Use 4 strips 2″ × 8½″ from those already cut if you are making *The Anniversary Sampler Quilt* (page 19). For any of the other quilts, please see their specific cutting instructions.

MAKE THE BLOCK

Seam allowances are ¼″ unless otherwise noted. Press all seams in the direction of the arrows indicated in the diagrams.

1. Referring to Oversized Half-Square Triangle Units (page 9), sew together medium red and cream 3″ triangles. Make 4. Press. Trim to 2½″.

2. Draw a diagonal line on wrong side of 4 dark red squares. Sew dark red square to corners of 4 cream rectangles. Press. Trim. See Folded Corners (page 10).

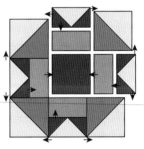

3. Sew together half-square triangle units, dark red 2½″ × 2½″ square, pink rectangles, and Flying Geese units. Press.

4. Frame the block with 4 medium green strips. Trim the block to 8½″ × 8½″. See Framing the Blocks (page 96).

The fun and funkiness of this block make me grin every time I make it. I like its sense of whimsy. Starry Path is a block I always choose to hand piece. It's one of those go-to blocks that I cut and stuff into my take-along sewing kit when I'm in between other hand-pieced projects. You can color this with just about anything, from primitive to contemporary fabrics, and it will always work.

MATERIALS

 Red print: 5″ × 7″ piece

 Medium pink print: 5″ × 7″ piece

 Light pink print: 6″ × 6″ square

 Cream solid: 8″ × 8″ square

CUTTING

Prepare templates from patterns T, U, V, and W (pullout page P1).

RED

◆ Cut 2 using Template T.

MEDIUM PINK

◆ Cut 2 using Template T.

LIGHT PINK

◆ Cut 4 using Template U.

CREAM

◆ Cut 4 using Template V.

◆ Cut 4 using Template W.

FRAMING STRIPS

◆ **Light green:** Use 4 strips 2″ × 8½″ from those already cut if you are making *The Anniversary Sampler Quilt* (page 19). For any of the other quilts, please see their specific cutting instructions.

MAKE THE BLOCK

Seam allowances are ¼″ unless otherwise noted. Press all seams in the direction of the arrows indicated in the diagrams.

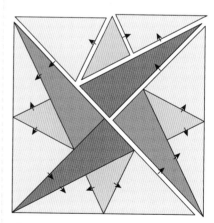

1. Sew together assorted pieces into triangular quarter-units. Press. Sew together quarter-units. Press.

2. Frame the block with 4 light green strips. Trim the block to 8½″ × 8½″. See Framing the Blocks (page 96).

Block 39: Eveningshades

The original version of this block is called Hope of Hartford. It's a good teaching block with its half- and quarter-square triangles and partial seams. But the best part about this block is the fun you can have playing with the corner rectangle by dividing it into different shapes. When you set the blocks straight together, all kinds of secondary things happen where the corners meet. Take a look at my quilt *Eveningshades* (page 89).

One bit of advice for this particular block is to use the finished-size Template X to mark and cut the elongated triangle shape. The cut size is a difficult measurement to rotary cut, and the template provides the necessary sewing lines to pin-match before stitching.

MATERIALS

 Red print: 4″ × 7″ square

 Pink print: 9″ × 9″ square

 Cream solid: 5″ × 10″ piece

CUTTING

Prepare a template from pattern X (pullout page P1).

RED

◆ Cut 2 squares 3⅛″ × 3⅛″. Cut each once on the diagonal.

PINK

◆ Cut 1 square 2″ × 2″.

◆ Cut 1 square 3½″ × 3½″. Cut twice on the diagonal.

◆ Cut 4 using Template X.

CREAM

◆ Cut 1 square 3½″ × 3½″. Cut twice on the diagonal.

◆ Cut 4 using Template X.

FRAMING STRIPS

◆ **Medium green:** Use 4 strips 2″ × 8½″ from those already cut if you are making *The Anniversary Sampler Quilt* (page 19). For any of the other quilts, please see their specific cutting instructions.

MAKE THE BLOCK

Seam allowances are ¼″ unless otherwise noted. Press all seams in the direction of the arrows indicated in the diagrams.

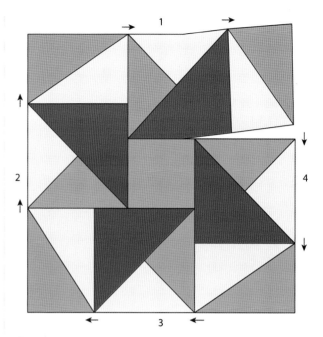

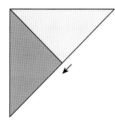

1. Pin-match points. Stitch together cream and pink pieces X. Unit should measure 2″ × 2¾″. Trim dog-ears. See Sewing Template-Marked Pieces (page 15).

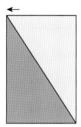

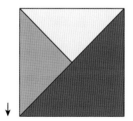

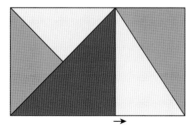

2. Sew together pink and cream quarter-square triangles. Sew to red half-square triangles. Sew a pieced rectangle to each. Press.

3. Use partial seams to sew units from Step 2 to sides of pink 2″ × 2″ square. See Partial Seams (page 18).

4. Frame the block with 4 medium green strips. Trim the block to 8½″ × 8½″. See Framing the Blocks (page 96).

Block 40: Key West Beauty

I often use Key West Beauty as a substitute for the LeMoyne Star block when teaching eight-pointed stars. Like the LeMoyne Star, you can fussy cut prints and patterns for the diamonds and spokes to create intriguing kaleidoscopic effects. This block, like its namesake in Florida, is great for playing.

Whether sewn by hand or machine, Key West Beauty is a breeze to make. It lends itself well to any fabric style from reproduction themes all the way to modern prints.

MATERIALS

 Red print: 4″ × 10″ piece

 Pink print: 7″ × 9″ piece

 **Cream solid:** 7″ × 9″ piece

CUTTING

Prepare templates from patterns Y, Z, and AA (pullout page P1).

RED
- Cut 4 using Template Y.

PINK
- Cut 4 using Template Z.

CREAM
- Cut 8 using Template AA.
- Cut 2 squares 2⅜″ × 2⅜″. Cut each once on the diagonal.

FRAMING STRIPS
- **Medium green:** Use 4 strips 2″ × 8½″ from those already cut if you are making *The Anniversary Sampler Quilt* (page 19). For any of the other quilts, please see their specific cutting instructions.

MAKE THE BLOCK

Seam allowances are ¼″ unless otherwise noted. Press all seams in the direction of the arrows indicated in the diagrams.

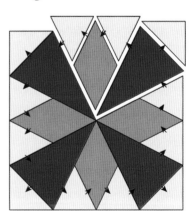

1. Sew a cream piece AA triangle to adjacent sides of a pink piece Z diamond. Press. Make 4. Sew a cream half-square triangle to end of each red piece Y spoke. Press. Make 4. Sew together units. Press.

2. Frame the block with 4 medium green strips. Trim the block to 8½″ × 8½″. See Framing the Blocks (page 96).

The Anniversary Sampler Quilt Assembly

Now that you have 80 blocks stitched, it's time to put the quilt top together. This quilt is composed of a medallion center, 4 quadrants of pieced blocks, 4 large pieced and appliquéd side setting triangles, and 4 large appliqué corner triangles.

Quilt assembly

If you look carefully at the photo of *The Anniversary Sampler Quilt*, you'll notice that some of the blocks are directional, meaning they have a top and bottom. Keep this in mind when you are positioning the directional blocks in the body of the quilt.

Refer to the quilt assembly diagram (page 95) while working through all the instructions (below). All border appliqué shapes and panels are on the pullout (pattern pullout pages P1 and P2).

FRAMING THE BLOCKS

After your blocks are done, it's time to frame them. The green 2″ × 8½″ strips are oversized so that you can trim all your blocks to a standard 8½″ after framing.

Use partial seams (page 18) to frame the block so that no matter how you rotate the blocks next to each other in the quilt, there won't be any framing seams to match.

MAKE THE MEDALLION CENTER

Medallion appliqué panel layout

1. Complete your dedication block with printing, embroidery, writing, photos, or something else.

2. Prepare the bias strips you've cut for vines. (I used a ¼″ Clover bias tape maker, spraying with Best Press as I ran the strips through the tool.) Cut them to fit as you need them (see Making Appliqué Stems, page 17).

3. Prepare the flowers and leaves using your preferred method of appliqué, whether for hand or machine.

4. Mark and appliqué 4 cream 8½″ × 8½″ squares using the appliqué panel 4 pattern. Sew them together alternately with the 2 A Piece of My Heart blocks and the 2 Dresden Plate blocks to make a big nine-patch center.

5. Trace the appliqué design for appliqué panels 2, 3 and 2R designs onto the 2 cream 8½″ × 24½″ border strips. Appliqué the vine into place, followed by the flowers and leaves. Use full-length vines where they will cross the seams onto the corners so you won't have to piece the vines. Do not attach any flowers or leaves that cross the seams until after you have sewn the side borders to the center nine-patch.

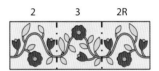

6. Trace the panels 1, 2, 3, 2R and 1R designs onto the 2 cream 8½″ × 40½″ borders. In the same fashion as the short borders, appliqué the vines, flowers, and leaves in place, leaving the corners free to connect after the border is sewn in place. Sew the long borders to the quilt center and finish appliquéing the pieces that cross the seams.

MAKE THE BLOCK QUADRANTS

Each quadrant is composed of 15 blocks laid out in 3 rows of 5 blocks each. The easiest way to make these is to repeat my block layout so that the medium and light frames alternate and the blocks are balanced across the quilt. I labeled the quadrants A, B, C, and D, with A being the one on the upper left side of the quilt. A and C have the same blocks in them; B and D are the same.

Sew the blocks into their respective quadrants. Pay attention to block direction when sewing the blocks into their quadrants.

MAKE THE OUTSIDE APPLIQUÉ

Make the Appliqué Side Setting Triangles

The side setting units are composed of smaller appliqué triangles sewn together with three pieced blocks. Appliqué the triangles along the edge of the quilt using panels 7 and 8.

1. Make 4 of panel 8.

2. Make 4 of panel 7 facing the same direction and 4 facing the other direction (7R) so the rose buds flow away from either side of panel 8.

3. Sew together these panels with the blocks shown in the diagram. As with the quadrants, the 4 side setting triangles sitting opposite each other in the quilt will have the same 3 pieced blocks in them.

Make the Appliqué Corners

1. Trim the corners of the large 8½″ × 16½″ cream rectangles. If you are working with a solid, you can cut 4 at the same time (there are 8 total). If you are working with a print, trim with 4 rectangles print side up and 4 print side down.

2. Place a ruler across the corner of stacked rectangles, with the 45° line on the long edge and the ½″ line bisecting the corner so that you will trim the corner ½″ larger. Trim the triangle away from the corner. These lopped rectangles are used to make appliqué panels 6 and 6R.

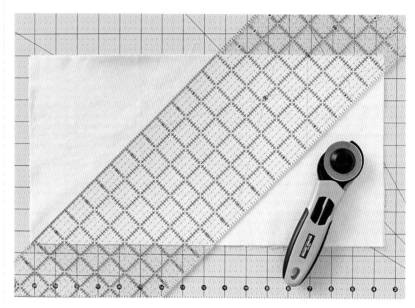

3. Using the big lopped cream rectangles, the 4 remaining framed blocks, and the big cream triangles, sew together the quilt corners. Using panels 5, 6, and 6R, mark the pieced corners with the appliqué design. Stitch the remaining flowers, vines, and leaves in place to complete the corners.

COMPLETE THE QUILT TOP

1. Sew the big side setting triangles to the sides of the 2 unattached block quadrants.

2. Add the units from Step 1 to the sides of the quilt center.

3. Sew the big appliqué corners to the top.

FINISH THE QUILT

1. Layer, baste, and quilt as desired.

2. Bind with the 2¼″-wide binding strips.

3. Prepare and attach a dedication label to the back of the quilt explaining who made the quilt, where, and when, along with the reason for the quilt.

Alternate Anniversary Quilt Sets

In the case that you don't want to make an 80-block quilt or you have a different anniversary or event to commemorate, this chapter contains alternate quilt sets for various year markers. You'll find quilt sets for 10-, 20-, 25-, 30-, 40-, and 50-year anniversaries. Each quilt set includes a diagram (without blocks), along with a sample made by a sewist using that set for her commemoration.

You're free to choose which blocks and how many of each you want to include in your quilt. In fact, you can choose just one block and make it as many times as you need to fill your quilt. For instance, if you want to make a quilt for a teacher celebrating 25 years in the profession, you might choose to make 25 Schoolhouse blocks in 1 color or assorted colors. Or if you love stars, you could make only the star blocks. The possibilities are as endless as your imagination.

Fabric requirements for each block are given with the individual block assembly instructions. Use this information as your guide for how much you need to make each block. If you are making multiples of the same block and using the same prints for all of them, multiply the fabric needed for 1 block by the number of blocks you are making. For instance, if you are making 5 of one block and you need a 5″ × 5″ square of the red print for a single block, you will need 5 squares each 5″ × 5″ for five blocks. A quarter yard (9″ × width of fabric) will be plenty from which to cut those 5″ × 5″ squares.

By the same token, multiply the quantities of pieces to cut for each print by the number of blocks you are making.

I piece my plain borders by cutting the strips and sewing them end to end into one long border strip. Then I measure and cut the individual border strips to fit the center width of the quilt. Let the seams fall randomly on the sides of the quilt, adjusting only if a seam is too close to the end of the border strip.

If you prefer a different method for making plain borders (such as using unpieced lengthwise grain strips), you will need to adjust the border yardages to accommodate your preferences.

You'll notice that some of the sample makers substituted quilting or embroidery for the appliqué in their quilts. Some added or subtracted borders or increased the number of prints used for the block frames. Why not?

Nor did the contributors always stick to the red-and-green color scheme of the original—they used everything from batiks to pastels to patriotic to reproduction. Anything goes! The samples were adapted to each quilter's preferences and creative ideas. Hopefully they will inspire you to come up with unique adaptations for your own treasure.

Some of the quilts have a blank block or a heart block in the center to be used for a dedication. These dedication blocks can be embellished with embroidery, signatures, hand written inscriptions, printed words, photos, a handprint, a drawing, or whatever else comes to your mind.

Be creative and commemorate your special event in a way that pleases you!

Ten-Year Anniversary

Finished quilt: 52″ × 61¼″

MATERIALS

Assorted red and pink prints: For blocks, as indicated in your chosen blocks

Cream solid: 1 yard for block piecing, as indicated in your chosen blocks

Medium green print: ½ yard for block frames

Light green print: ⅜ yard for block frames

Light red print: 1½ yards for side setting triangles

Red print: ¾ yard for vertical sashes and inner border

Pink print: ⅞ yard for outer border

Binding: ½ yard

Backing: 3½ yards (with horizontal seam)

Batting: 60″ × 69″

CUTTING

Refer to your chosen blocks for individual block cutting instructions.

WOF = width of fabric

MEDIUM GREEN

◆ Cut 6 strips 2″ × WOF; subcut into 24 strips 2″ × 8½″.

LIGHT GREEN

◆ Cut 5 strips 2″ × WOF; subcut into 20 strips 2″ × 8½″.

LIGHT RED

◆ Cut 2 strip 13″ × WOF; subcut into 4 squares 13″ × 13″. Cut each twice on the diagonal.

◆ Cut 2 strips 7″ × WOF; subcut into 6 squares 7″ × 7″. Cut each once on the diagonal.

◆ Cut 1 strip 6⅛″ × WOF; subcut into 2 pieces 6⅛″ × 11⅞″.

RED

◆ Cut 3 strips 2″ × WOF.

◆ Cut 5 strips 3″ × WOF.

PINK

◆ Cut 5 strips 5½″ × WOF.

BINDING

◆ Cut 7 strips 2¼″ × WOF.

Construction

Seam allowances are ¼″ unless otherwise noted.

Block Assembly

Make your choice of 10 blocks. Referring to Framing the Blocks (page 96), frame 6 blocks with medium green strips and 4 blocks with light green strips.

Make the Quilt Top

Press all seams in the directions of the arrows indicated in the diagram.

1. Cut a 6½″ × 6½″ square of cream solid for the dedication block. Frame the block with the light green print.

2. Sew 2 blocks, the dedication block, 4 light red half-square triangles, and 4 light red quarter-square triangles into the center vertical strip as shown in the quilt assembly diagram (below). Add a light red rectangle to the top and bottom edges.

3. Sew together the remaining blocks, light red quarter-square triangles, and light red half-square triangles to make the second and third vertical strip, as shown.

4. Sew together the vertical strips, vertical sashes, and borders as shown.

Quilt assembly

Finish the Quilt

Layer, quilt as desired, and bind.

Susan's Victory Garden by Beth Woods, machine quilted by Denise Mariano, 52″ × 61¼″

Beth's beautiful quilt was made for her sister to celebrate 10 years of being cancer free. What a joyous reason to make a quilt! Her choice of black for her block backgrounds, combined with happy solids, is heart lifting.

Finished quilt: 48¼″ × 48¼″

MATERIALS

Assorted red and pink prints: For blocks, as indicated in your chosen blocks

Assorted reds: To equal ¼ yard for appliqué

Assorted pinks: To equal ¼ yard for appliqué

Cream solid: 3 yards for appliqué in this quilt *and* block piecing as indicated in your chosen blocks

Medium green print: 1 yard for block frames and appliqué leaves

Light green print: ¾ yard for block frames and appliqué leaves

Dark green print: ⅜ yard for vines and appliqué leaves

Red print: ⅝ yard for border and binding

Fusible webbing: 18″ × 1½ yards

Backing: 3 yards

Batting: 56″ × 56″

CUTTING

Refer to your chosen blocks for individual block cutting instructions.

Prepare templates from patterns BB, CC, DD, EE, FF, and GG (pullout page P2).

WOF = width of fabric

MEDIUM GREEN

- ◆ Cut 2 strips 8½″ × WOF; subcut into 40 strips 2″ × 8½″.
- ◆ Cut 1 strip 1⅞″ × WOF; subcut into 4 strips 1⅞″ × 10½″.
- ◆ Reserve the remainder for cutting appliqué leaves.

LIGHT GREEN

- ◆ Cut 12 strips 8½″ × WOF; subcut into 40 strips 2″ × 8½″.
- ◆ Reserve the remainder for cutting appliqué leaves.

DARK GREEN

- ◆ Cut 1 piece 11″ × WOF for bias stems.
- ◆ Reserve the remainder for cutting appliqué leaves.

CREAM

- ◆ Cut 3 strips 8½″ × WOF; subcut into 2 strips 8½″ × 16½″ and 2 strips 8½″ × 32½″.
- ◆ Cut 1 square 8⅜″ × 8⅜″ for dedication block.
- ◆ Cut 2 squares 9″ × 9″. Cut each once on the diagonal.
- ◆ Reserve the remainder for block piecing.

RED

- ◆ Cut 2 strips 1″ × WOF.
- ◆ Cut 5 strips 2¼″ × WOF.

ASSORTED LEFTOVER GREEN PRINTS

- ◆ Cut 16 using Template CC.
- ◆ Cut 44 using Template DD.

ASSORTED REDS

- ◆ Cut 12 using Template BB.
- ◆ Cut 20 using Template EE.

Cutting continues on page 102.

Cutting continued.

ASSORTED PINKS

◆ Cut 12 using Template GG.

◆ Cut 20 using Template FF.

Construction

Seam allowances are ¼" unless otherwise noted.

Block Assembly

Make your choice of 20 blocks. Referring to Framing the Blocks (page 96), frame 10 blocks with medium green strips and 10 blocks with light green strips.

Make the Quilt Top

Press all seams in the directions of the arrows indicated in the diagram.

1. Frame the 8⅜" × 8⅜" cream square with the 1⅞" framing strips; then add the 9" half-square triangles to make the center medallion. Trim to 15½", including seam allowances. Sew the 1" red strips to all 4 sides of the medallion.

2. Use appliqué panels 1 and 2 to appliqué the cream border strips.

3. Sew together the blocks, appliqué borders, and medallion center as shown.

Quilt assembly

Finish the Quilt

Layer, quilt as desired, and bind.

Simple French by Cynthia Ann Burgess, machine quilted by Denise Mariano, 48¼" × 48¼"

Ann chose her favorite blocks and made them multiple times to celebrate her twenty years of quilting. She substituted beautiful quilting in place of the appliqué. She pulled the majority of her fabrics from her large collection of French General prints by Moda.

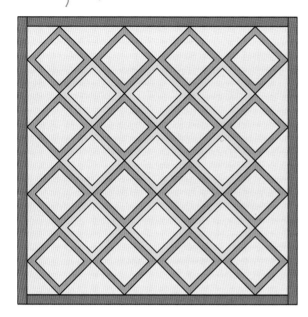

Finished quilt: 49¾″ × 49¾″

MATERIALS

Assorted red and pink prints: For blocks, as indicated in your chosen blocks

Cream solid: 2⅜ yards for block piecing and setting triangles

Medium green print: 1 yard for block frames

Light green print: ⅝ yard for block frames

Red print: ½ yard for outer border

Binding: ½ yard

Backing: 3 yards

Batting: 57″ × 57″

CUTTING

Refer to your chosen blocks for individual block cutting instructions.

WOF = width of fabric

MEDIUM GREEN

◆ Cut 4 strips 8½″ × WOF; subcut into 64 strips 2″ × 8½″.

LIGHT GREEN

◆ Cut 2 strips 8½″ × WOF; subcut into 36 strips 2″ × 8½″.

CREAM

◆ Cut 1 strip 13″ × WOF; subcut into 3 squares 13″ × 13″. Cut each twice on the diagonal.

◆ Cut 1 strip 7″ × WOF; subcut into 2 squares 7″ × 7″. Cut each once on the diagonal.

◆ Reserve the remainder for block piecing.

RED

◆ Cut 5 strips 2½″ × WOF.

BINDING

◆ Cut 5 strips 2¼″ × WOF.

Construction

Seam allowances are ¼" unless otherwise noted.

Block Assembly

Make your choice of 25 blocks. Referring to Framing the Blocks (page 96), frame 16 of the blocks with medium green strips and 9 with light green strips.

Make the Quilt Top

Press all seams in the directions of the arrows indicated in the diagram.

Sew together the blocks, side setting triangles, and corner triangles as shown. Add the borders.

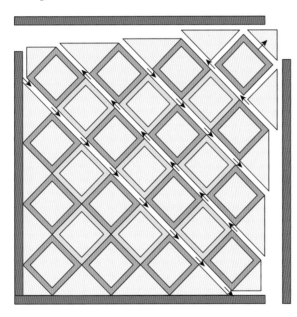

Quilt assembly

Finish the Quilt

Layer, quilt as desired, and bind.

For Michelle by Doris Brown, machine quilted by Denise Mariano, 49¾" × 49¾"

Doris proudly made this quilt for her daughter Michelle to celebrate what seemed like 25 years of college! Each block has a special meaning for the journey of this young, working single mom, who despite many travails stuck with her goal. Doris used more than just 2 sashing prints and substituted the owl batik for the cream in the side setting triangles as a tribute to Michelle's college mascot. Congratulations, Doris and Michelle!

Thirty-Year Anniversary

Finished quilt: 66½″ × 68¾″

MATERIALS

Assorted red and pink prints: For blocks, as indicated in your chosen blocks

Cream solid: 2 yards for block piecing

Green print: ⅝ yard for vertical sashes

Pink print: 1⅝ yards for setting triangles

Red print: 1⅛ yards for outer border

Light print: ¾ yard for inner border

Binding: ½ yard

Backing: 4 yards

Batting: 74″ × 76″

CUTTING

Refer to your chosen blocks for individual block cutting instructions.

WOF = width of fabric

GREEN

◆ Cut 10 strips 2″ × WOF.

PINK

◆ Cut 4 strips 10″ × WOF; subcut into 13 squares 10″ × 10″. Cut each square twice on the diagonal. You will have 2 leftover triangles.

◆ Cut 2 strips 5½″ × WOF; subcut into 10 squares 5½″ × 5½″. Cut each square once on the diagonal.

RED

◆ Cut 7 strips 5″ × WOF.

LIGHT

◆ Cut 7 strips 3″ × WOF.

BINDING

◆ Cut 7 strips 2¼″ × WOF.

Construction

Seam allowances are ¼" unless otherwise noted.

Block Assembly

Make your choice of 30 blocks.

Make the Quilt Top

Press all seams in the directions of the arrows indicated in the diagram.

1. Sew the blocks into 5 vertical strips using the quarter-square and half-square triangles.

2. Trim the rows to ¼" from the points.

3. Join together the rows with the green vertical sashes.

4. Sew the inner and outer borders to the quilt center.

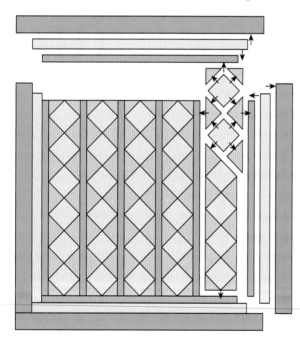

Quilt assembly

Finish the Quilt

Layer, quilt as desired, and bind.

Thirty Shining Stars by Donna Lynn Thomas, machine quilted by Theresa Ward, 66" × 68½"

I made this quilt to commemorate the many quilters who helped or influenced me over the years. I chose 6 star blocks and made 5 of each for a total of 30 blocks. The beautiful soft red, teal, and brown prints are from Jo Morton's Gratitude collection for Moda. The light-brown side setting triangles are from Barbara Eikmeier's Waddington Road collection for Paintbrush Studio.

Forty-Year Anniversary

Finished quilt: 74″ × 74″

MATERIALS

Assorted red and pink prints: For blocks, as indicated in your chosen blocks

Cream solid: 3⅞ yards for block piecing and borders

Medium green print: 1⅜ yards for block frames

Light green print: 1¼ yards for block frames

Red print: ½ yard for border

Pink print: 1⅜ yards for border

Binding: ⅝ yard

Backing: 5 yards

Batting: 85″ × 85″

CUTTING

Refer to your chosen blocks for individual block cutting instructions.

WOF = width of fabric

MEDIUM GREEN

◆ Cut 5 strips 8½″ × WOF; subcut into 84 strips 2″ × 8½″.

LIGHT GREEN

◆ Cut 4 strips 8½″ × WOF; subcut into 80 strips 2″ × 8½″.

CREAM

◆ Cut 5 strips 3¾″ × WOF for borders 1 and 3.

◆ Cut 6 strips 3½″ × WOF for border 4.

◆ Cut 1 square 6½″ × 6½″ for dedication block.

◆ Reserve the remainder for block piecing.

RED

◆ Cut 7 strips 2″ × WOF for border 5.

◆ Cut 4 squares 2″ × 2″.

PINK

◆ Cut 8 strips 5″ × WOF for border 6.

◆ Cut 2 strips 2″ × WOF for border 2.

BINDING

◆ Cut 8 strips 2¼″ × WOF.

Construction

Seam allowances are ¼″ unless otherwise noted.

Block Assembly

Make your choice of 40 blocks. Referring to Framing the Blocks (page 96), frame the dedication block and 20 of the blocks with medium green strips. Frame 20 blocks with light green strips.

Making the Quilt Top

Press all seams in the directions of the arrows indicated in the diagram.

1. Referring to the quilt assembly diagram (below), add red framing strips to the dedication block. Sew the red and cream borders around the dedication block.

2. Sew together the blocks and center.

3. Add the assorted borders.

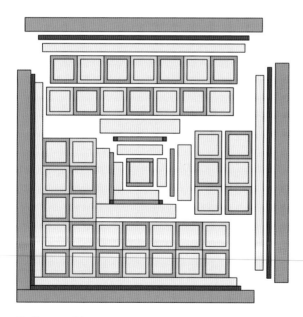

Quilt assembly

Finish the Quilt

Layer, quilt as desired, and bind.

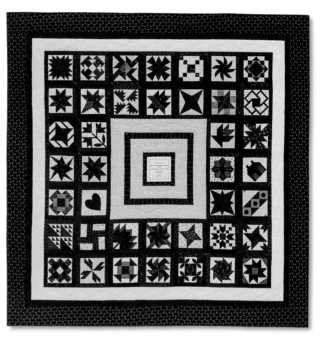

Forty Years Ago by Donna Lynn Thomas and Barbara J. Eikmeier, machine quilted by Theresa Ward, 2016

My friend Barb and I joined forces to help make one of these quilts for each other in order to honor our husbands' military service. We chose red, white, and blue as the color theme and each made 2 sets of 20 blocks for both our own quilt and to contribute to the other's quilt. This quilt belongs to me. Although long retired from the Army, my husband Terry was commissioned in 1977, 40 years ago.

Fifty-Year Anniversary

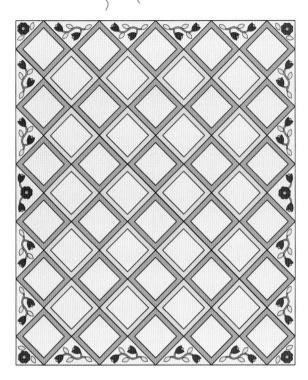

Finished quilt: 57″ × 68⅜″

MATERIALS

Assorted red and pink prints: For appliqué in this quilt *and* for blocks as indicated in your chosen blocks

Cream solid: 4½ yards for block piecing and setting triangles

Medium green print: 1⅞ yards for block frames

Light green print: 1¼ yards for block frames

Dark green print: ⅜ yard for vines and appliqué leaves

Assorted green prints: 1 yard total for appliqué leaves

Fusible webbing: 18″ × 1¼ yards

Binding: ⅝ yard

Backing: 4 yards (with horizontal seam)

Batting: 65″ × 76″

CUTTING

Refer to your chosen blocks for individual block cutting instructions.

Prepare templates from patterns BB, DD, EE, FF, and GG (pullout page P2).

WOF = width of fabric

MEDIUM GREEN
- Cut 6 strips 8½″ × WOF; subcut into 120 strips 2″ × 8½″.

LIGHT GREEN
- Cut 4 strips 8½″ × WOF; subcut into 80 strips 2″ × 8½″.

CREAM
- Cut 2 strips 13″ × WOF; subcut into 5 squares 13″ × 13″. Cut each twice on the diagonal.
- Cut 1 strip 7″ × WOF; subcut into 2 squares 7″ × 7″. Cut each once on the diagonal.
- Reserve the remainder for block piecing.

DARK GREEN
- Cut 1 piece 11″ × WOF; subcut into 12 bias strips ¾″ wide.
- Reserve the leftovers for appliqué leaves.

ASSORTED REDS
- Cut 32 using Template EE.
- Cut 8 using Template BB.

ASSORTED PINKS
- Cut 32 using Template FF.
- Cut 8 using Template GG.

ASSORTED GREENS
- Cut 56 using Template DD.

BINDING
- Cut 7 strips 2¼″ × WOF.

Construction

Seam allowances are ¼″ unless otherwise noted.

Block Assembly

Make your choice of 50 blocks. Referring to Framing the Blocks (page 96), frame 30 blocks with medium green strips and 20 with light green strips. Make your dedication block 1 of the 50, and add it in a central position.

Make the Quilt Top

Press all seams in the directions of the arrows indicated in the diagram.

1. Use panels 7, 7R, and 8 to appliqué the side setting triangles. Appliqué a single rose with 2 small leaves in the 4 quilt corner triangles.

2. Sew together the blocks and appliquéd side setting triangles as shown.

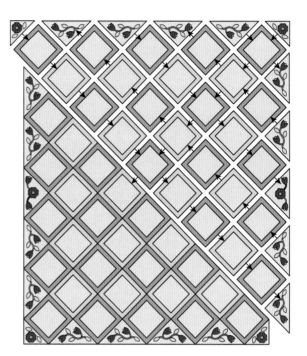

Quilt assembly

Finish the Quilt

Layer, quilt as desired, and bind.

Alice used lovely light-hearted pastels to make a very feminine quilt commemorating a lifetime of happy memories. A master at hand embroidery, she chose to embroider the appliqué design instead of appliquéing it in the side setting triangles. She made all 40 blocks and made 10 of her favorites a second time to make 50 blocks in all.

Sweet Memories by Alice M. Clark, machine quilted by Denise Mariano, 57″ × 68⅜″

About the Author

Donna Lynn Thomas has been sewing since the age of four and passionately quilting since 1975. She began teaching in 1981. As an Army wife, she lived in Germany for four years, where she thoroughly enjoyed teaching at a quilt shop and various guilds throughout the country. Long out of the Army, the Thomases have settled in Kansas. Donna continues to teach and speak nationally.

Donna places a strong focus on mastering basic and precision skills to help quilters reduce their frustration and better enjoy the creative process. An author of quilt books since the late 1980s, Donna continues to write and contribute articles to various quilt-related publications. You can find her column, "Quilting Fundamentals," in *Modern Quilts Unlimited*.

Donna designed the Omnigrip On Point Ruler and its companion ruler, the On Point Square. These rulers give you the ability to cut pieces that measure neatly on the diagonal, eliminating the messy math usually involved in setting patchwork units on point inside blocks or borders.

Donna's greatest joy is her husband, Terry, and their two sons, Joe and Pete. Equally dear to her heart is Joe's wife, Katie, and Donna's most-perfect-in-every-way granddaughters, Charlotte and Alexandra.

Donna and Terry provide staff assistance to their two cats, Max and Skittles, and a kiddie pool and ear scratches to one sunny golden retriever, Ellie. All the quilts in their house are lovingly "pre-furred."

Follow Donna on social media:

Website: donnalynnthomasquilter.com

Facebook: /donnalynnthomasquilter

Instagram: @dtdonna55

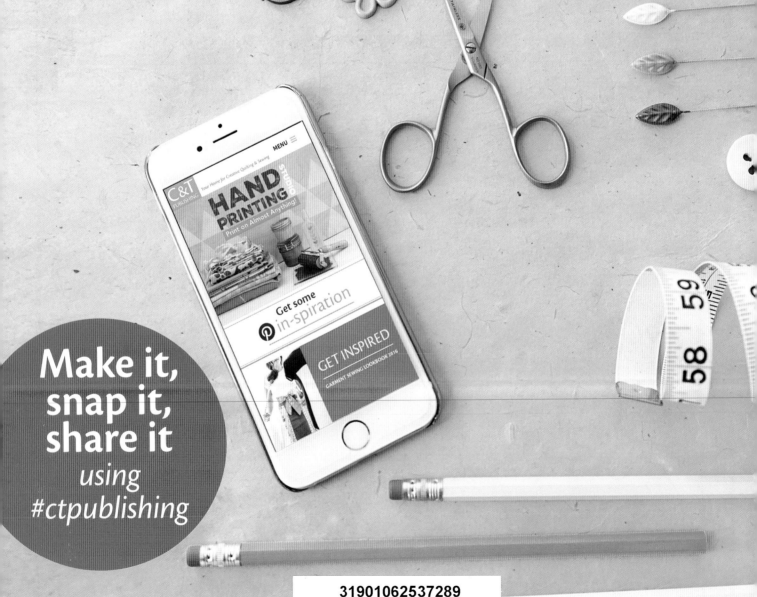

Want even more creative content?

Go to ctpub.com/offer

& sign up to receive our gift to you!

Make it, snap it, share it *using #ctpublishing*

31901062537289